All About
VARMINT
HUNTING

All About

Photographs & text

Distributed by Stackpole Books
Cameron and Kelker Streets
Harrisburg, Pennsylvania 17105

VARMINT HUNTING

by Nick Sisley

THE STONE WALL PRESS, INC.
1241 30th Street, N.W.
Washington, D.C. 20007

Cover crow photograph by Luther C. Goldman, Courtesy of U.S. Fish and Wildlife Service.

Cover preparation by Kim F. Hasten.

Library of Congress Cataloging in Publication Data:
Catalog Card No. 82-060946
Sisley, Nick
All About Varmint Hunting

ISBN 0-913276-41-3

Printed in the United States of America.

Contents

Photo Credits

Page 39: Courtesy of Remington Arms Co.
Page 43: Courtesy of Remington Arms Co.
Page 46: Courtesy of Sturm, Ruger and Company, Inc.
Page 46: Courtesy of Sturm, Ruger and Company, Inc.
Page 70-top: Courtesy of Weaver Optics
Page 70-second: Courtesy of Weaver Optics
Page 70-third: Courtesy of Bushnell Scopes
Page 70-bottom: Courtesy of Bushnell Scopes
Page 72: Courtesy of Redfield Scopes
Page 74: Courtesy of Lyman Scopes
Page 77: Weaver Reticles, courtesy of Weaver Optics

All other photography by the author.

Introduction

This book is intended to fill a void. Varmint hunting and varmint hunters have been cheated through the history of outdoor literature. Proportionate to their numbers and to the amount of money they spend, varmint hunters have come up on the short end of the stick with regard to ink covering what they love to do. This has been particularly true in the outdoor book realm, but it is also true with regard to the general interest outdoor magazines. The only places the varmint hunter can read and learn about varmint hunting are a few special interest magazines. Even these tend to give minimal amounts of space to this popular sport.

While *ALL ABOUT VARMINT HUNTING* isn't meant to be the last word, it has been designed to cover all facets of this unique sport, and to give in-depth coverage. Woodchucks are given by far the most space. This is because there are so many individuals caught up in this sport these days. There's more interest here than with any other species. You'll find woodchuck shooting covered from A to Z.

Prairie dogs have an extensive chapter devoted to them. Fox hunting is given a special chapter; then comes the final book section on shotgunning varmints such as crows, pigeons and pest starlings. To my knowledge *ALL ABOUT VARMINT HUNTING* encompasses more about the "breadth of the sport" than any previous work.

I hope you enjoy it.

Good Shooting,

Nick Sisley
The Summer of 1982

CHAPTER 1

The Woodchuck:
The Rifleman's Best Varmint Target

Summertime is the off season for most riflemen, a period when days off work are spent mowing grass, listening to ball games, taking the Mrs. shopping, weeding gardens, pruning shrubs, painting ceilings, and cleaning out garages. Daydreams fill such outdoorsmen's visions this time of year; visions about getting a rifle in their hands and easing through the winter woods trying to get a whitetail buck in the cross-wires, or perhaps working along a canyon rim looking for mule deer signs.

The sportsman who has been afflicted with a summer disease commonly known as chuck fever doesn't have to deal with those uninteresting summer chores too often, nor does he have to dream much about future days afield, because he can grab a rifle off his gun rack most any summer day. The woodchuck, *Marmota monax,* is out there waiting to be caught in a scope sight. In many areas of the country this furry little varmint exists in plentiful numbers.

While this book deals with all manner of varmints, many of which can be hunted year 'round, the majority of its pages are devoted to the woodchuck, for this is the critter more and more hunters are seeking these past two decades. They're seeking chucks during the summer, the off season for most any other rifle sport. Before delving deeply into the various ways of hunting them: special rifles, cartridges, scopes, bullets, accuracy tips, wind doping and more, it's important to learn as much as possible about this creature we're going to be

1

pursuing so often in future summers. A great amount of what follows in this chapter is somewhat scientific in nature. I'll make those scientifics as readable and enjoyable for you as possible. Only by learning a great deal about the quarry we're after can we become so-called experts. As much as field and shooting experience will help you become more of an expert chuck hunter, what you're going to learn in this chapter is just as essential—if not more. Future chapters will revolve around hunting experience, ballistics, and hunting how-to. Those ensuing chapters may interest you more. Still, this chapter is essential. If you'll keep an open mind, you'll learn a great deal.

The woodchuck or ground hog is indigenous to much of the country, especially the highly populated east and midwest. While some of the best chuck hunting states are New York, Pennsylvania, West Virginia, Virginia, Maryland, Kentucky and Tennessee, these summer targets also exist in plentiful numbers in all or parts of Maine, New Hampshire, Vermont, Connecticut, Massachusetts, New Jersey, Delaware, North and South Carolina, Georgia, Alabama, Arkansas, Missouri, Indiana, Ohio, Illinois, Iowa, Michigan, Wisconsin, Minnesota, North and South Dakota, and small portions of several other states.

Male woodchucks typically emerge from their winter burrows in early February. Famous Punxsutawney Phil traditionally comes out February 2 in central Pennsylvania—to let the world know how long winter is going to last. If Phil the Predicter sees his shadow you can bet we're going to have six more weeks of winter, or so the sages say. If Phil doesn't see that shadow, spring weather is just around the corner—only two weeks away. All this makes good newspaper copy and fine TV news segment stuff, but male woodchucks emerge in early February for specific reasons. Mainly, they're staking out their territory and become very feisty with other males of the species. The younger males travel, finding and establishing a territory for themselves. The females don't emerge from hibernation until three or four weeks later. By then the males have their territories well defined, so the ladies of the clan don't have to put up with their brawling shenanigans.

The emergence dates I have given have been verified by game biologist R. L. Snyder in an extensive study (done for his doctorate thesis) conducted in south-central Pennsylvania. Emergence dates may vary in other parts of the country (i.e. earlier to the south, later to the north). I doubt the dates would vary much.

Most breeding activity takes place the second and third week in March. Since the female's gestation period lasts for 32 days, the young are usually born the second and third week of April. Snyder discovered that the young stay underground for about thirty days before emerging topside, which means the little chucks begin seeing sunshine around May 15. By the end of the third week in May the little ones are weaned.

They're still not on their own, though. Mother Chuck protects them for several more weeks against their main natural predator—foxes. She probably also teaches her young about caution, foraging, and other necessities for survival.

The average female chuck will have just under four little ones. This average naturally varies with a number of factors, some of which we know about, most of which we can only speculate. Females two years and older become pregnant almost one hundred percent of the time. Only twenty percent of the year-olds might become pregnant in normal populations, but the incidence of pregnancy in these younger female chucks varies with a number of factors. If fewer older females are available, the males are naturally going to be more inclined to woo the youngsters, perhaps nature's way of resecuring proper age balance. If there are as many or more mature females as there are males to breed, the young females probably won't get pregnant until the following spring.

Each chuck hunter must always deal with the ethical question, "When can I begin hunting chucks each season?" There are no pat answers. To be certain, the young chucks should be capable of caring for themselves before you take the chance of shooting their mother. Hold off hunting until around the first of July, or at least until after the first hay cutting. However, some chucks exist in pastures and fields which are seldom, if ever, cut. If these chucks aren't hunted before the vegetation gets too high, like in April and the first two-thirds of May, they can't be hunted later in the season. Chucks existing in this latter type of territory are certainly in the minority. Some states have had and currently have a season on chucks; usually a season that's closed in the spring. Here there's no ethical question for the hunter to answer for himself—he must abide by the law.

The ethical question is compounded in some areas by extremely dense ground hog populations. There's little question that in some parts of their habitat chucks become so plentiful that they cause problems. Too many burrows can mean broken legs for livestock, crippled farm machinery that plunge into those burrows, even serious injury and death to farmers who operate that machinery. More than a few bib-overalled, tobacco chewing tractor operators have met their Maker when their rig overturned because of a tire dropping into an extra large chuck excavation. I know one area of one state (no, I won't name it) where I concentrate summer hunting. There's a familiar reply when I stop at the farmhouse to ask permission to hunt. Usually it goes like this:

"Ground hogs! You wanna hunt ground hogs? Yeah, go ahead. Kill every one of those ¢ñs$*£+¢#&*$!!" It's true—where chucks are super plentiful, farmers detest them. Such concentrations are the exception, not the rule. In such areas it may be ethical to hunt chucks in the spring of the year, but that decision will have to be an individual one, unless the law precludes hunting them.

July and August are always excellent months to pursue Mr. and Mrs. Woodchuck. These are the months when farmers mow their hay fields and when the quarry is exposed to a hunter with a good rifle. Once September arrives, the chuck is inclined to become more lethargic. Later in September they're above ground even less. The vast majority of woodchucks have gone into their burrows by October first (not my opinion—scientific fact). Sure, maybe you've seen chucks out in October, maybe even later. R.L. Snyder discovered that these animals are still above ground because they haven't taken on enough fat stores yet. Often something else is physically wrong with them. These late foraging chucks have considerably less chance of making it through the winter.

Fat storage is extremely important for ground hogs. Snyder found that a chuck needs a minimal amount of fat stored if that animal is expected to make it through the winter. Without that minimum reserve their chances of getting through hibernation are significantly reduced—thus the sighting of the occasional chuck above ground in October, sometimes even in early November.

The males have fat reserves still left even when they come out of hibernation. This reserve helps them re-establish their breeding territory, fend off challenging males, and the fat store helps them get through the reproductive process. They eat almost nothing until reproduction is completed. Females emerge from the dens with less fat reserve because they emerge later. Yet they need significant fat reserves to aid them through pregnancy and lactation of the little ones.

Young chucks don't put on much fat until mid-September. Almost everything they eat during the summer is used to increase their growth. During the last two weeks of September, the young chuck's body takes on a dramatic fat increase. On the other hand, mature chucks begin building their fat stores sooner, but slower. By mid-July, stores in the older animals begin to build, but the last two weeks of September means a tremendous change in fat content for them as well.

Woodchucks appear to grow every year, though the most significant degree of growth takes place in the first two years of their life. Snyder handled over 1,700 woodchucks in his study (which took place on ten thousand acres of the Letterkenny Army Ordnance Depot near Chambersburg in southcentral Pennsylvania), and the biggest chuck he ever saw weighed 15 pounds 2 ounces, a male he trapped on September 4. That animal weighed 9 pounds 9 ounces the next March 5—when it was recaptured. The largest female Snyder came in contact with spun his scale needle to 12 pounds 11 ounces. This was one weighed on August 28. So—male chucks do grow bigger than females. This may not be so with regard to young of the year. The largest yearling Snyder ever weighed was a female on September 28—8 pounds 12 ounces, while the largest male of the year showed up in one of his traps on the same date—an 8 pound 10 ouncer.

When you shoot a chuck and walk out to the kill site, you probably pick the critter up, admire it, check to see what the bullet did, confirm how close you came to your aiming spot, etc. You might be interested in how old the chuck is. How can you tell?

Early in the season—late May through June, it's easy to tell the youngsters that are only weeks old. They're considerably smaller than any others. At birth a chuck'll weigh thirty to thirty-five grams, which translates to about one ounce—doggone small. By the time they are weaned, a chuck will weigh in the neighborhood of 1¼ to 1½ pounds. My mid June they'll average over two pounds, closer to 2½. By the end of June they're almost three pounds. Pretty easy to tell a chuck this small from one born the previous year or before.

A chuck born the previous year will weigh over 2,000 grams when it comes out of hibernation—about 4½ pounds. By mid July, however, a few chucks born that spring, if extremely healthy, will weigh as much as the smallest chucks born the previous year, so it then becomes increasingly difficult to tell a mature chuck from one of the year—if one tries to determine this fact by weight alone.

There is another way. Check the chuck's prominent incisor teeth. By midsummer even the chucks that were born the previous spring will begin to show a brownish stain on these incisors. When chucks emerge from their dens in the spring, those born the previous year will not yet have these stains, though they do accumulate the brown stains by mid July or shortly thereafter. The incisors of the young are also narrow and pointed compared to the older chucks, which become broader as the points wear off with age. Remember that the woodchuck is from the rodent family, a characteristic of which is continual growth of these incisors, growth that has to be cropped by the animal.

So if you kill a chuck before midsummer, it's easy to tell by weight whether it was born that same spring or not. If the animal weighs more than 4½ pounds prior to midsummer, but has no brown staining on the incisors, it was born the previous spring. If it weighs at least 4½ pounds and has brown stained incisors, you've killed a chuck that was born at least two springs previously. After midsummer, weight can't be relied on. Then you can only check the incisors to determine age—brown stains mean born some previous spring—lack of brown staining means the chuck was born that same spring.

Unlike some animals and birds, chucks only have one litter per year. Robert Snyder didn't find any pregnant females after April 21. Sex ratio between males and females is normally 1:1. From June onward, young chucks of the year gain weight at the rate of about twenty grams per day (a little over half an ounce). By hibernation time they'll weigh

Non-stained incisors of sub-adult woodchuck.

roughly three thousand grams (approximately 6½ pounds). Chucks born the previous spring (year-and-a-half old at time of hibernation) will weigh closer to five thousand grams (around eleven pounds). With this latter group there is much more variance in weight than with the other two groups—young of the year and year-and-a-half olds.

One of the main purposes of Robert Snyder's doctorate study was to determine if removal of female chucks from a known population could affect reproductivity of that population. In studies with animals other than woodchucks, removal of a significant number of females could cause considerable social stress among the remaining animals. Reproduction would be severely affected. Snyder discovered this is also the case with chucks.

One tract on Letterkenny Army Depot (none of this area was open to public hunting, so it was naturally an excellent area for a controlled experiment like this) was set aside by Snyder for removal of females. This was done mainly by box trapping. The trapped males were immediately released (for the most part), while the trapped females were either removed and transported to another area or sacrificed for further scientific study.

This removal of females on the specified tract took place over a course of two years, 1957 and 1958. We laymen might be quick to

6

jump to the conclusion that nature would cure this problem that Snyder had purposely set up—with more mature females moving into the area, more males moving out, increased birth of females compared to males, etc. Some of this did occur. However Snyder's primary finding was the 1959 birth rate went way down. In just two years of considerable female removal, the average litter size went from just under four youngsters to just under three youngsters. The birth rate went from 1.11 to .51. Why?

The increased competition among the males for fewer available females perhaps had some effect on the reduced birth rate, but it appears this isn't the controlling factor. The available female chucks *were* impregnated by the males. Loss of the young during pregnancy was *the* major factor in the population decline.

Why are these young lost? Females, apparently feeling the increased social stress, go through endocrine or hormone changes that cause them to abort far more than they would under normal population conditions. On a nearby study site at Letterkenny, Snyder randomly killed a tremendous number of chucks, without regard to sex. Every year this population would bounce back remarkably well, females showing perhaps even less tendency than normal to abort during pregnancy.

What does all this mean? The lowly woodchuck has been used for some unique scientific findings, and he's being used now for even more research. Today Robert Snyder heads up the research team of the Penrose Research Laboratory, which is in conjunction with the Zoological Society of Philadelphia, and the University of Pennsylvania. He uses chucks all the time as test animals.

What else has the scientific community learned from woodchucks? First, they can act as a replacement for chimpanzees in numerous studies. Chimps are on the endangered list these days, but they helped man conquer polio. Today chucks are being used to help man wage its war against cancer.

Twenty-five percent of the woodchucks at the Penrose Laboratory have contracted liver cancer. Tumors begin to show up on a chuck's liver two to four years after that chuck has had a bout with hepatitis. Cancer begins to grow significantly in man ten to thirty years after the initial insult. Because the hepatitis that chucks contract is so similar to at least one type of hepatitis that humans contract, researchers hope to develop a vaccine to prevent cancer of the liver—all this because the chuck's onset of liver cancer surfaces so much sooner after a bout with hepatitis.

It hasn't yet been proven that hepatitis in man can cause cancer, but it has been proven in lower primates. The circumstantial evidence that hepatitis either does or can cause human cancer continues to build. Only the scientists know what the future holds for woodchucks in scientific research. This furry little varmint that summer riflemen seek in their scopes might have an important role.

Woodchucks are not nocturnal. Like most humans, they sleep at night and forage for at least part of the day. Some say they feed morning and evening, but my experience has been they tend to feed much more during this second period than the first. This might be due to the fact that many summer mornings result in dew covered grass and hay. I'm of the opinion that chucks aren't especially fond of getting wet. Sure, I've gunned them in even a light drizzle, but the few times this has happened has been following a period of extremely hot weather, extremely dry weather, or both. It's my guess the animals are merely out and foraging, maybe just enjoying the slightly cooler temperatures that accompany rain, and/or they're so darn glad to see a drought end. On the standard summer morning with plenty of dew covering the vegetation, you won't find many chucks walking about the clover.

By midday or shortly thereafter, you can expect chucks to be above ground, maybe for several hours on the typical summer day. This period, right up until near sundown, is when the summer hunter should be afield.

During the warm months, chucks don't tend to move around much. They have their territories established, so unless something dramatic happens to make them change, they stay within self-imposed boundaries. In the spring, young woodchucks tend to move around considerably. No doubt this is nature's way of helping them find their niche in the world. There is some movement in the late fall as well.

Being subterranean critters, they tend to prefer soil types that drain well, shale being one of their favorites. Many burrows go underground for a couple of feet, then the little caves are dug upward, sometimes in a fairly complicated labyrinth. Almost every ground hog den has at least two entrances. One is usually what some hunters call a "peep hole." This is a hole that comes straight up out of the ground, rather than slanting inward at an angle. No doubt peep holes are dug from below, while most of the slanting burrow entrances are dug beginning at topside.

Some might think that these animals have strong hind legs, for they sometimes see chucks flinging loose dirt quite a distance with those back legs when they're digging. However, a chuck's front legs are much stronger, and these are the ones he uses for digging. The hind legs merely remove the loose dirt that the front ones have excavated.

Chucks can become extremely wary animals if under heavy hunting pressure, but they're not nearly so vigilant where hunted minimally. They'll retreat from most any danger, but if cornered they make surprisingly good fighters. A farm dog with plenty of experience dispatching chucks has no problem, but a canine new to the task will have his hands (paws?) full with a mature woodchuck. Foxes would almost

An unusual albino woodchuck.

certainly have to take a mature chuck by surprise to be successful, but there's little question these secretive predators are capable of doing that. Besides man and farm dogs, foxes are about the only predator a chuck has to fear, at least that's true over most of its range.

While photographing chucks one spring I spent an entire afternoon clicking the shutter on one animal. Several times he ventured from his burrow, waited while I focused, checked the light meter, and exposed considerable film. But he kept ending each session by going back in his burrow. Evidently the chuck was hungry. After coming out for the fourth or fifth time, he scurried away from the hole, running as fast as he could, out of sight over the top of a little crest that was only ten or fifteen yards away.

My initial thought was the chuck figured it was too dangerous to stay at that hole any longer—with that strange looking critter (me) intruding on his domain. He was hightailing it for greener pastures. But I wasn't sure. Consequently, I crept slowly and silently to the den, then followed up the hill to see if I could determine what happened. I worked with extreme slowness, not wanting to spook this chuck in case I did come upon him. If I could keep him above ground a bit longer, it'd mean more photos—and with a different background.

Finally I spotted that chuck, and he was feeding hungrily, like he was making up for lost time. The timothy was several inches high, so only his back was showing when he was horizontal and feeding. By moving only when the chuck was down, and with painstakingly slow and silent movements, I crept closer and closer—on my belly. The chuck was only about thirty yards away when I peeked above the crest, but eventually I cut the distance to half of that. Then I cut the distance in half again. Still, the quarry didn't spot me. Finally, when I was only three or four yards away and was focusing my camera, the ground hog spotted me out of the corner of his eye. He wouldn't look directly at me, but crouched lower. I expected a mad dash escape attempt, but it didn't happen—maybe because I was between the chuck and the safety of his underground burrow.

While I watched and took pictures, the chuck sank lower and lower. There was no question this critter was "playing 'possum'!" I stood fully erect, taking more pictures. The photos weren't saleable because this chuck didn't look natural—lying flat to the ground. I circled the chuck once, twice, then again. The camera lens was within a yard of his nose, but that chuck hardly quivered a muscle. I ended up walking away, but the last I saw him he still hadn't moved. Bet he scampered back to his burrow not long after I vanished from sight, though.

Had I made any attempt to get close enough that the chuck figured there was imminent danger, I'm certain he'd have put up his dukes for a fight. Knowing that, I didn't bother challenging him. It was both an unusual and a rewarding experience.

There are a number of different color phases in woodchucks—very dark, yellowish, reddish, probably several other shades. There are a few albinos. I've seen one—check the photo. I've heard of one black or melanistic phase chuck. These are probably extremely rare. Still, the average woodchuck is grizzled on his top parts, lighter on his underparts. The young have a blackish head compared to adults.

The little varmints have a great deal of vitality, even after they're hit with bullets that break up instantly. There is a theory that one thousand foot pounds of energy are necessary to kill something the size of a whitetail deer, assuming the bullet strikes some critical area of the animal. While the average deer weighs a hundred pounds or more, the chuck weighs ten pounds or less. It wouldn't be too far out of order to claim that a ten pound chuck would take approximately one hundred foot pounds of energy—for a clean kill with a bullet placed in a lethal area. The fact of the matter is most summer riflemen hunt chucks with centerfire weapons that far exceed one hundred foot pounds in energy at the striking distance.

Even the puny 17 Remington has about four hundred foot pounds of energy at two hundred yards. Hitting a chuck with a little 17 at that range would be comparable to hitting a whitetail with four thousand foot pounds—and a 340 Weatherby Magnum only produces about three thousand foot pounds of energy at two hundred yards. The popular 222 Remington dispatches about six hundred foot pounds at two hundred yards, the 22-250 eight to nine hundred, the 6mm Remington up to 1,500 with a ninety grain bullet. No wonder chucks are killed so quickly with the average centerfire.

Chucks will occasionally escape to the hole if hit by a centerfire. This is never the problem of too little bullet energy remaining, but always the problem of a poorly placed shot, one that doesn't strike the chest, neck or head. The average woodchuck can escape to his burrow even if hit with a well placed 22 rimfire slug. The reason for this is minimal energy. A 22 long rifle hollow point only has about 156 foot pounds of energy at the muzzle, 85 foot pounds at one hundred yards. That figure is under the one hundred pound minimum I've suggested for a ten pound chuck. Even if hit squarely in the chest with a 22 long rifle hollow point, instant death is unlikely. Though essentially dead on his feet, a chuck might still struggle back into its den, just as a whitetail with its heart or lungs shot out might travel a surprising number of yards before keeling over.

The little 5mm Remington Magnum stretches things considerably further than the 22 long rifle. Muzzle energy of this fast stepper is about 375 foot pounds. Even out to 150 yards the little 38 grain pill retains over 165 foot pounds of energy, what a high velocity 22 rim starts out with. Muzzle velocity with the 5mm Remington Magnum is over 2,100 feet per second. This is a great little short range chuck rifle, and we'll talk about it more in a future chapter, but only one 5mm rifle was ever produced by Remington, their Model 591. Alas, Remington no longer offers the rifle. Evidently the cartridge will die, too—the only bottleneck rimfire ever.

With the last few paragraphs I've made a transition of setting the stage—moving away from woodchuck scientifics toward woodchuck hunting. I hope you've learned something from this first chapter, at least about the animal. Next we'll talk about hunting him, and the necessary equipment.

With their rifle rig in front, on a Cravner Rest, these two gunners glass for long range woodchucks.

CHAPTER 2

Hunting Woodchucks

Standard Long Range

Within the last ten or fifteen years, long range shooting is the type of varmint hunting that has become more and more popular with riflemen. Woodchucking saw its first true devotees when the 22 Hornet centerfire extended the range of the 22 rimfire—from an estimated hundred yards max to about a hundred and fifty.With cartridge innovations, more outdoorsmen enjoyed shooting ground hogs at the maximum distance for each new cartridge. With the advent of the 222 Remington, literally thousands of would-be rifle buffs became confirmed chuck hunters. While a few potted pigs at long distances in the '30's and '40's with 22-250 Varminters and 220 Swifts, multitudes began killing chucks at ranges of 250 yards with the 222. Since the 1950 introduction of the "deuce," the varmint hunting multitudes have begun messing with even longer range cartridges and weapons—the even flatter shooting 22 centerfires, the "6's," and the 25's. While 250 yards was a long shot in 1952 for the multitudes of hunters, thousands upon thousands today take shots at 275, 300, 350, even the occasional 400 yard try. Long range woodchuck hunting has come a long way!

Today's version of long range requires an extremely flat shooting rifle. Trajectory that's on a rope out to about 350 yards is what today's chuck hunter opts for. The 22-250 Varminter is ideal for this gunning, and that cartridge is available in an unusually wide variety of bolt action rifles, plus the Ruger Number One Single Shot and its Browning counterpart. Many gun manufacturers market both standard barrel and heavy barrel versions in 22-250.

For the chuckmaster interested in bigger calibers, there's a variety of 243's and 6mm Remingtons from which to choose. Because of increased recoil (slight) with these two popular pig cartridges, the heavy barrel versions will often make the best choice for summer precision shooting. The 25-06 is available for this long range gunning, too. Several manufacturers offer a choice of standard or heavy barrel. This writer suggests the bull tube job.

If one isn't currently outfitted for standard long range chuck gunning, how does he go about selecting the proper equipment? Much of this book is devoted to that question, but since this chapter deals with what so many readers will deem of higher interest, let's zero in on several suggestions. The four calibers mentioned, the 22-250, the 243 Winchester, the 6mm Remington, and the 25-06 are all ideal for this long range gunning at the ranges specified. There are others, and a writer is always open to criticism if he doesn't mention someone's favorite chuck ordnance in a treatise like this. There's no denying that there are numerous excellent cartridges for the 275 to 400 yard precision this chapter covers, but the four specified are readily available. You can check one of them out at practically any shooting emporium you venture into. When it comes to price on one of these standard long range weapons, your bank roll will not be totally depleted. Also, since there's so much ready availability, there's always a good chance to haggle to make sure you get the best possible deal.

The Remington 700, Ruger 77, Winchester 70, and Smith & Wesson 1500 offer most or all of the four cartridges mentioned, in some cases in either standard or heavy barrel versions. The same might also be said for several imports—Sako, Steyr-Mannlicher, Parker-Hale, etc. Standard version barrels in most or all four calibers are available from Alpine, Savage, Browning, Harrington & Richardson, Kleinguenther, Interarms, Weatherby and a few others. The American buyer is always interested in choice, mainly because a wide choice means competition, and competition means fairer consumer pricing and continual improvement in quality.

An entire chapter in this book is devoted to scopes, and the potential long range chuck shooter needs to make a thoughtful and effective scope sight choice. It would be tough to make a wrong selection if one opted for a 10X or 12X in a scope of high quality. Fine or extra fine crosshairs should be selected for the reticle in a scope used for this specific purpose.

You'll also need handloading equipment. The proper yet inexpensive tools required to produce first quality reloads will save you money in the long run, and you can tailor your bullet and powder load combination for the chuck rifle that you'll use. The more varmint shooting you do, the more you'll save. Factory ammo has recently been escalating appreciably in cost. The cost of reloading ammo has also been going up, but not in relation to how fast factory fodder is increasing.

Quality binoculars are absolutely essential to standard long range shooting. There's no way the average sportsmen's eyes will be able to pick out varmint size targets at 300 yards and beyond. Let me qualify that. A person with 20/20 vision can easily pick out a standing or moving chuck in a bare hay field, but these chucks are a small percentage of the ones shot at by experienced hunters. A quality binocular permits picking out chuck heads as they peak from their holes, or chuck backs that are down and feeding in alfalfa, clover and/or timothy that might be several inches high or higher. Learning how to glass carefully, effectively, and for long periods is a major part of becoming an expert varmint shooter.

Rounding out this chuck hunter's needs is a firm, steady rest from which to shoot those distant targets. At the ranges we're talking about, off-hand, even prone shooting without a rest, should not even be tried. Gents interested in long range are too conscious of precision.

Precision is what long range shooting is all about. When a genuine chuck hunter wraps himself around a 6mm Remington 700 Varminter with heavy barrel, he's not thinking about bagging that chuck, as a trophy hunter might level the sights on a Dall sheep he's already envisioning over his mantel. The chuck hunter is, instead, totally conscious of shot placement. Rather than watching crosswires bob all over a deer's chest, as in off-hand holding, the chuckster is watching almost perfectly steady crosswires, and they're leveled on a very small part of a very small critter—maybe an eye, a puny neck, even the ear hole. He's conscious of the wind on his face, wind out where the chuck is, wind in between. He has carefully judged the range, hopefully to within ten or fifteen yards. He knows precisely what the trajectory of his bullet is from point blank to four hundred yards, and exactly where the bullet will strike at the range he has estimated this chuck at being.

This precision, this attention to detail, is what long range chuck shooting is striving to attain. Bagging the animal is not of major consequence. In fact, if this chuck hunter whizzes his 55 grain Sierra within a whisker of the chuck's ear, there's some sense of accomplishment. The shooter knows he's done a great deal right to be able to place his projectile so precisely. The fact that woodchucks are varmints, cause damage to crops, and are many times more abundant than they should be all adds up to more support for chuck hunting.

The hunter described in this chapter typically gets away from his vehicle. There may be times when he sets up in close proximity to his car, but those occasions will be the exception, not the rule. Being on the move a great deal means the binoculars he carries, the rest he

This gunner levels on a "long range" chuck with a Savage 112V in 220 Swift. Rest on fore-end is Harris Bipod.

uses to steady his hold, even the rifle/scope rig over his shoulder must be within reasonable weight limitations. I suggest twenty five ounces max for binoculars, a rest like the Harris Bipod (the smaller of two models available only weighs nine ounces), and a rifle/scope rig that doesn't go over eleven pounds. The weight of the latter is considerably more than one would want for most big game hunting, but chuck hunts usually take place over terrain that isn't too difficult to traverse. Plenty of time is spent sitting and glassing from advantageous viewing points.

The chuck hunter on the move is able to get back away from hard surface and dirt roads where many tyros tend to concentrate their efforts. Getting to glass and closely observe fields that are off the beaten path usually means more shooting action. The chucks won't be as wary either.

This hunter might spend all afternoon glassing one huge parcel of chuck territory, or he may move several times so he can scan the binoculars across new terrain. This will depend upon how much action you find. Two buddies working together, one spotting each shot for the other, is the most effective procedure. Scope black out after most shots usually prevents the shooter from seeing exactly where his bullet strikes. In the event of a miss by the rifleman, his buddy with the binoculars calls, "High five inches, a tad left, too." The man in the prone position quickly feeds in another cartridge, makes those adjustments with his hold, and assuming the chuck is still there, makes a second shot—hopefully a telling one.

The precision one achieves through continually working at the long range game, in conjunction with a close companion, is only one benefit. These experiences tend to become a rifle shooter's most treasured memories. The long shots I've made and missed, and those of a few of my companions in this sport are savored often: Arch Hulings with Swift or 270—both Pre-64 Model 70 Winchesters, "Skin" Doutt with his Pre-64 243 Winchester, Don Lewis with a vast array of chuck getters, the first varmint rifle that ever graced my wall rack—a 243 with Douglas barrel on a Mauser 98 action, shooting with a number of 25-06's I've owned in the past and some I own yet today.

Shooting farther and farther is the current state of the art! Today's highly accurate factory rifles (at least some of them), the ease of reloading precision ammo, the outstanding quality scopes now available, the binoculars, the rests all add up to scoring with distance shots that were once unheard of. Additionally, the long shots of yesteryear have become so easy today that some veteran pig hunters don't even bother shooting at those minimal distances because they consider the ranges unsporting.

Is this standard long range varmint hunting the pinnacle of the sport? Or are we likely to see increasing numbers of hunters trying even longer shots in the future—even scoring with at least some degree of regularity? I think so. Super long range shooting, four hundred yards and far beyond, may never appeal tomorrow to as many thousands as standard long range varminting appeals to today, but sportsmen who become enamoured with super long range are bound to increase. There are some in this latter group who are already calling shots of 250 yards too easy. They don't bother shooting because they know any chuck squeezed on at that range is a goner. *Marmota* doesn't have a chance. These gents are developing the technology required for even more precision, for having better and better chances of producing killing shots at four hundred yards and much farther.

Before going into a discussion of super long range varmint hunting, let's first take a close look at this next section about improving your big game hunting ability on chucks, for there are thousands who will be interested. You will then be better prepared (or have your appetite whetted) for the section on "Super Long Range."

To Improve Big Game Hunting

For every hunter who picks up a varmint gun to have a try at summer woodchucks, there a thousand who take to the woods every fall in hopes of bringing back a deer. This isn't mentioned to put varmint hunters on the defensive since they're outnumbered, because almost every chuck hunter of the summer is a deer hunter come fall. One of the best ways to sharpen deer hunting skills, and to handle a deer rifle with total confidence and more expertise, is to use that same rifle (or at least the same model in a varmint caliber) all summer long on chuck hunts.

Many skills contribute to bringing home the venison consistently. Some of these skills are moving slowly and cautiously, seeing a broad array of landscape and making sure it is devoid of game before going on, moving silently, moving in parts of the landscape where keenly observant game will be less likely to see you, the ability to fire off hand when required—with dispatch and accuracy, reading signs game have left behind, making use of saplings for shooting stability and more.

To some degree, all these skills can be at least partially honed during the summer. All it takes will be time, effort, and your deer rifle. In case the big game rifle you're currently using is available in a varmint caliber, you might want to make another gun investment. For instance, if you have a Remington 788 bolt gun in 308 Winchester for deer, you might want to try the 243 Winchester for summer chucks. Both have the 18½ inch barrel. If you have a Remington 700 in 270 Winchester (or any of the many other suitable deer cartridges in which the 700 is available), you might want to try a 700 in 17 Remington, 222 Remington, or 22-250. The options with many other bolt action models are similar—Ruger 77, Winchester 70, Smith & Wesson 1500 and several others.

If you decide to sling your deer rifle over your shoulder, you might want to try some different loads. Most bullets intended to perform properly on deer size game won't expand quickly enough on the smallish groundhog. Say you fire, in 6mm caliber cartridge, the 100 grain Sierra semi-pointed for deer. For chucks switch to the 100 Spitzer Boat Tail or one of Sierra's 85 grainers, the Spitzer, or the Hollow Point Boat Tail. If you're shooting a 120 grain bullet in your 257 Roberts or 25-06 for deer, switch to the sharply pointed 100 grain Sierra for chucks. If you shoot 140 grain balls at deer with your 264 Winchester Magnum, try the 120 Sierra for chucks. If you're a 270 man shooting either 130 or 150 grain bullets at deer, consider the 110 grain Sierra Spitzer for the summer season. If you can locate any 130 grain Remington Bronze Points in 270 caliber, you'll find them excellent on

Standing and glassing—chuck hunters interested in improving big game skills tend to stay on the move.

either chucks or deer size game. Unfortunately, Remington has stopped selling bullets to reloaders.

There are many 7mm cartridges, and they're all used on deer. I predict the 7mm's are going to become even more popular for big game in the future. The 140 grain bullet is optimal for deer size game in this caliber, whether you're carrying a 7 × 57 Mauser, a 284 Remington, a 7mm-08, a 7mm Express or a 7mm Remington Mag. For chucks, however, drop that 140 grain back to either the 120 grain Sierra Spitzer or the 115 grain Speer Hollow Point.

Perhaps the 30 caliber is the most popular one for deer. The 150 and 180 grain bullets might be chambered for 90 percent of the nation's fall deer hunts. For chucks there are a wide range of lighter bullet possibilities—like the 125 grain from Sierra, the 110 Spire Point from Speer and the 110 Spire Point from Hornady.

The reloading manuals from the three bullet companies mentioned provide excellent data for stuffing any of the mentioned bullets. Where possible, I suggest not loading the lighter bullets to absolute maximum velocity if you're trying to hone your deer hunting skills. Rather, if you can still come up with a safe, recommended load, try to come close to duplicating the velocity of the load you use for deer. By doing so you'll come closer to matching trajectories. If all your deer shots are at close range, this suggestion will have less importance.

While the most typical summer chucking involves carefully selecting a stand and waiting out the quarry until it emerges topside, I suggest on the move hunting for chucksters interested in honing big game skills. Taking up a stand is a fine way to bag a whitetail effectively, but stand hunting doesn't really involve all that much hunting skill—and honing hunting skills is what you're trying to accomplish if you're wanting to put the theory behind this chapter into practice.

Learn to move slowly and cautiously on summer jaunts, for that's exactly the way you'll have to hunt in the fall if you expect to still hunt deer with any hope for success. Learn patience. Don't let the afternoon become a contest to find out how much ground you can cover. *The object should always be to spot the game before it spots you.* Fail to do that, even if you eventually shoot that particular woodchuck, and you've missed out on one of the most important aspects of consistently successful big game hunting. Game that's totally unaware of your presence is relatively easy to put a telling bullet into. Once game suspects or knows of your presence, it's likely to be on the move, less likely to provide the easy shot. In many instances, spooked game (chucks or deer) vanishes before a shot can be taken.

Chucks are not nearly as wary as whitetails. Thus they provide good training. We can make more mistakes with chucks and still score; so it keeps our interest up. A hog hunter with a big game rifle over his shoulder will encounter his share of fairly close shots, maybe even

A chuck has been spotted. The hunter stays low to keep out of sight and uses the woods' edge to hide his movements.

those of twenty-five yards or less. At ranges up to a hundred yards, sometimes even a tad more, off hand shooting will often be required—that's if a closer approach is impossible and if the intervening terrain prevents getting lower to use the kneeling, sitting, or prone position. The basic game plan for the chuck hunter dedicated to improving big game skills, however, should be to spot the quarry before it spots him; then plan and make a stalk, a stalk that takes him within the most reasonable distance that insures a telling shot.

I've made stalks on lowly woodchucks that took over an hour; this because I had to make a wide circle to get into the proper position. Naturally such long stalks are the exception, not the rule. Sometimes after putting all that time and effort into a stalk, I get to where the chuck was and he's gone—either already loaded down with clover and alfalfa, or I've spooked the critter somewhere during my stalk. The same thing could happen in British Columbia when hunting stone sheep!

Whether you're trying to spot the first chuck of the day or making a stalk, the same essentials are there: move slowly, silently, keeping low and away from the skyline. Because woodchucks are hunted in open spaces, it's particularly important to move slowly as you approach each little crest. With every step, new, previously unobserved chuck territory comes into view. One of the easiest ways to spook an un-suspecting ground hog is to move too quickly in this circumstance.

During the early 1960's I did a tremendous amount of chuck hunting with this philosophy—improving my skills with regard to big game. I made it a rule never to shoot at chucks that were beyond three hundred yards. If shooting at that self-imposed maximum distance or close to it, I always used a good portable rest and fired from the prone position, just as I would if taking a three hundred yard shot at a mulie across a Montana canyon. Any time I spotted a chuck that didn't see me first, the primary objective was, "Can I get closer? If so, how?"

In whitetail hunting, getting closer during a still hunt is almost never called for. It's spot the deer, hopefully before it spots you, then get off a quick accurate shot before moving even one step further. With most other big game hunting, especially hunting that takes place in reasonably open terrain, the closer stalk is what the challenge is all about. Closer stalks haven't been as necessary the last fifteen or twenty years—as they were much earlier in big game hunting history. That's because so many of today's hunters carry rifles that are so powerful and flat shooting. Still, stalking puts the "hunt" back into hunting. All of us can benefit from becoming better stalkers. The experiences one can derive, whether stalking a barren ground caribou or lowly *Marmota monax,* can be richly rewarding.

Frankly, I'm not much for off-hand shooting. Even so, I practice off-hand religiously prior to each deer season, knowing that if I get a shot at a whitetail, there's a good chance I'll have to take it off-hand. Summer chuck hunters who want to improve their off-hand big game skills should do a lot of off-hand shooting at little woodchucks each June, July and August. One of the greatest shots I can remember making was with my little 5mm Remington rimfire. With the puny 38 grain bullet I drilled a chuck through the head at a long, counted 118 steps— off-hand! I'd be the first to admit a great deal of luck was involved in that one, but I was trying to accomplish exactly what I did accomplish. The 5mm can't be considered a big game rifle, but I was hunting on the move, and I did make a long stalk to get as close to this chuck as possible. I couldn't get closer and there were no rests available. I had to stand fully erect to be able to see him. The point is that a great off-hand shot at slightly more than a hundred yards can be just as satisfying as a five hundred yard shot with a super heavy rig made for ultra long range, firing from a solid rest and the prone position. By shooting off-hand repeatedly during the summer, the hunter can't help but improve his abilities when a buck presents itself for one of those typical quick shots when either no rest is available, there's no time to take one, or both.

Whether or not to tote some type of rest, hunting chucks with the philosophy espoused in this chapter must be left with the individual. I tend to lean toward one, but admit that I've never carried a similar rest on a whitetail hunt. I might, however, consider doing so on a big game hunt in which long ranges were expected and open country would be hunted (i.e., antelope, certain mule deer habitat, sheep, barren ground caribou, etc.).

I've spoken elsewhere in this book about a rest I particularly like, the Harris Bi-Pod, which attaches ingeniously to the front swivel stud of a rifle. I find the Harris Bi-Pod extremely good. Sometimes I even use it on the bench to fire excellent groups, though bench resters might giggle up their sleeve since the Bi-Pod might not permit "straight-line" recoil, something bench resters shooting one hole groups are extremely interested in. Few other rests are as convenient, adjustable, light and stable as the Harris.

Another I've used for years is a pointed rod that fits inside a piece of tubing, with some type of wingnut to lock the pointed rod in position with relation to the tubing (for raising and lowering), and some type of padded "U" on top in which to rest the rifle's fore-end. This light-weight rest is carried on a snap attached to my belt loop.

Another suggestion is one I adapted from Bob Cassidy's rest idea, two pieces of wood attached via a pair of hinges, a "U" notch on top to rest the rifle's fore-end during shooting. Yet another is the "walking stick." An entire section is devoted to rests for chuck hunting, so it isn't the province of these paragraphs to delve too deeply. Suffice to say, if you feel a rest is in order for summer chucking, but you still want to emphasize improvement of big game skills, you must opt for a very lightweight rest. Since you'll be on the move almost continually, a super stable set up will not only be out of the question from a weight standpoint, it'll be unwarranted since almost all your shots will be within reasonable range anyway.

I can understand a philosophy of **not** carrying any type of rest if the individual is strictly trying to simulate big game conditions and situations. Using that no-rest philosophy, the hunter is going to have to do a great deal of shooting from the off-hand position, plus make use of trees, saplings, fence posts, etc., to better stabilize those cross-hairs on all but the closest of targets.

Whether using a rest or not, the hunter sneaking around is going to sight a lot of woodchucks that will require moving in bent over

23

positions and/or crawling on hands and knees. This will be required to put the shooter in a position so he can use his rest from the prone or kneeling position, or use the prone or sitting position without a rest. The rolling contours of the land dictate attempting closer approaches from a low, bent over position time after time. Be willing to crawl around summer hay fields, even if you sometimes feel a bit silly.

Every fall millions of hunters take to the woods after deer. No wonder the whitetail is the nation's Number One Big Game Animal. He has earned that right. One way to put yourself a cut above the average deer hunter is to concentrate improving your stalking, hunting and shooting skills during the summer period—by getting out after that furry little varmint more and more are coming to recognize as *Marmota monax.*

Super Long Range

Bob Cassidy got me interested in super long range shooting, and my transition didn't take place all that long ago. I consider standard long range to be in the vicinity of 350 yards, super long range to be 500 yardish stuff. Bob lives less than a half hour away. We met through our mutual October and November interest in grouse and woodcock. On one of our upland hunts we discovered each other's mutual love for varmint hunting. Prior to sampling Cassidy's version of chucking, my version consisted of picking any one of a myriad of rather light rifles from the wall rack, affixing a makeshift rest to my belt, grabbing a pair of binoculars, and heading out the road a few miles.

I usually stayed on the move, though at times I'd glass large areas for a half hour, maybe less. Chucks were taken at twenty-five paces—on out to about three hundred yards. The latter I considered maximum on ethical grounds. I felt that if my bullet didn't have a chance to kill the chuck I was after, I should either stalk my way into closer range or pass up the shot.

Cassidy's philosophy was at odds with mine. His was to hunt right from where he parked his vehicle, using rifle and scope combinations that were too heavy for carrying. Bob only took shots at chucks that were far beyond what I considered max distance. He used special rests that couldn't be carried either, but with those rests it was possible to fire groups as small as when firing from a bench at the shooting range.

In only a few years I was able to garner a great deal of information on this extra long range varminting, almost all of it through hunting with and interrogating Bob Cassidy. I tried shooting with factory heavy barreled 25-06's of various gender for this super long range work, but in no way could they match Cassidy's performance with his heavier rigs. He was certainly more precise than I with his equipment.

This is a super long range shot—approximately 600 yards to the extreme corner of the distant field.

Through telling you about the type of equipment I've seen him use over the years while we've shared hayfield shooting together, you'll learn what you will need to become effective at the ranges I'm talking about. Bob and I regularly shoot at chucks that are 450, 500, 550, even 600 yards. Last summer I paced off the distance to one chuck Cassidy killed—686 long ones. The summer before I paced off the distance to a brace of chucks he bagged—on succeeding shots no less. They were poleaxed at 578 and 592 paces—long steps that would simulate yards.

Though Cassidy has more than three heavy varmint rifles, I've only ever seen him use this trio. His oldest and perhaps favorite is a 25-06 with super heavy stainless steel barrel on a Mauser 98 action. Cassidy figures he has used this one to try over 2,500 woodchucks. It is topped with a Unertl 15X Ultra Varmint scope (two inch objective lens for lots of light gathering). The 25-06 shoots 100 grain Sierras at max velocity with Hodgdon 4831 powder.

The day Bob killed that brace of chucks on succeeding shots, 578 and 592 paces, he was wrapped around his 6mm-284. This one uses a .284 Winchester case necked down to 6mm and firing 85 gr. Sierra HPBT bullets. A fast stepper, this one is extremely flat, but the bullet isn't quite as heavy as that 100 grain Sierra he uses in the 25-06. Consequently, the 6mm-284's wind bucking powers aren't quite as great. Bob has used this rifle plenty, but he doesn't have nearly as much experience with it as he does with the 25-06. The 6mm-284 is also fitted with a Unertl Ultra Varmint scope.

Bob's most recent acquisition for summer long range shooting is a 6.5mm-06. In this one he uses the 120 grain Nosler Solid Base. Again maximum loads of 4831 (Hodgdons) are stuffed in the case. Since Bob has considerable love for the 25-06 he's not ready to claim this 6.5-06 is better for super long range, but I have an idea that, in time, he's going to say it is the epitome for what he's trying to achieve at super long range. The Unertl Ultra Varmint scope also tops this rig off. The bull barrel measures 1⅛ inches from stem to stern, and it's 28 inches long.

The wood on all Bob's guns is massive. Each outfit will spin a scale needle past fifteen pounds. All are probably capable of ½ minute five shot groups, though Bob claims the varmint hunter needs accuracy only half that good. His rest, covered more thoroughly later in this book, is the most stable I've ever shot from. It consists of two pieces of an industrial hardboard called micarta, put together with hinges for raising and lowering and something sharp in the bottom of the rest so it'll dig in when placed on the ground. A "U" is shaped in between the hinges where a sand bag is placed. The rifle's fore-end goes here. Another sand bag is under the rifle's butt. This set up results in holds that are as solid as those capable from the best of bench rests.

Anyone interested in trying chucks at ranges beyond what are today considered standard long range, should invest in equipment that's capable of performing at these extreme distances, as Cassidy has. Trying shots at 500 yards requires far more precision than that required of 350 yard shooting. At 500 yards a max velocity bullet might drop almost three feet below the crosswires, even if sighted in for 250 yards. At 350 that same bullet might only be six or seven inches low. Be 100 yards off in guessing 500 yards and the bullet won't even come close to the target. It sure is easy to make the mistake of judging 450 when the range is actually 550, or vice versa.

Wind also becomes a major factor at 500 compared to 350. In only a ten mph crosswind a 90 grain from a 25-06 will drift around thirteen inches at 350 yards. It's reasonably easy to judge that distance in the scope. At 500 yards that bullet will drift almost three feet, and three feet isn't easy to judge in any scope. How is all this extra precision achieved?

First off, Cassidy uses the flattest shooting cartridges he can find. To help develop max loads he uses extremely strong cases. The 284 Winchester is noted for its strength. So is the 270 Winchester, which is very close dimensionally with the 30-06. Consequently, when having his chambers bored out, Cassidy opts for the 270 dimensions and uses the 270 case to neck down instead of the 30-06. The latter was developed to handle chamber pressures of 50,000 psi, while the 270 is made to withstand pressures of 54,000 psi.

Bob buys the heaviest, most expensive barrels he can find. Because he isn't shooting 22 caliber centerfires, his larger calibers come back with more recoil. The heft of his rigs, heavy barrel, dense, ample walnut, results in negligible recoil. Heavy weapons also sit the bags with extreme steadiness.

Bob feels the Unertl Ultra Varmint scope is the best he can buy— outstanding optics, and loads of light gathering ability with that two inch objective lens. He also has some of these scopes outfitted with one or two extra crosswires below the main reference wire; so he can hold more precisely at the extreme ranges. His perfectly steady rest is a major contributor to his precision shooting.

Bob never hunts alone. He's always with someone who will call his shots. Without an assistant, scope blackout prevents him from seeing where the bullet strikes on many occasions. If the shot misses, and most of them will at 500 yards, and he doesn't know where the bullet went, he doesn't have a clue about where to hold for following shots, or how or what he might have misjudged for that first shot—wind, range, etc.

Finding areas where long shots are possible isn't all that easy, especially long shooting that one can drive the vehicle to, for Cassidy's heavy rifle rigs don't permit carrying. Some areas of the country won't even offer 500 yard shooting, for there are few if any vistas where one can overlook good hayfield habitat at those distances. In flat agricultural land it will almost always be impossible to see that far.

With farm crops so valuable these days, there are fewer and fewer alfalfa, clover and timothy fields. Grain crops produce considerably more cash, so grain is taking over from hay, especially in relatively flat areas. Chucks are still thriving in hillier country, steep side hills where farmers wouldn't think of taking machinery that costs five and six figures. Here cattle or dairy herds are pastured, and vintage tractors with well worn haymaking equipment work the slopes, mowing the winter supply of food for the livestock. Where dairy farms abound so do woodchucks, and the hillier the terrain where the Holsteins and the Guernseys forage, the higher the woodchuck population is likely to be.

In many instances the super long range hunter can set up with a vista across a valley, shooting from one hillside into the opposing hill. Cassidy and I have a number of farms where we can experience this type of distant shooting. We reach most of them by unimproved farm road and set up our rifle rigs in the fields just off the roads. Many times we glass from the roof of the vehicle, our binoculars atop cylindrical sand bags for added stability—needed in long term viewing. Sometimes we find excellent hunting away from the dirt road, right in the farmer's fields. Many times we're successfully able to obtain permission to drive our vehicle over the farmer's tractor lanes until we can pull off at a strategic location where we can park the car, set up the rifles on their rests, and begin our glassing.

It's particularly rewarding to hunt country with long vistas and lots of chucks. Each day we spend in a top area we can average twenty-five to thirty super long range shots—each! Volume shooting like this is nothing compared to prairie dog gunning, but, in the highly populated east, this type of shooting—today—must be considered excellent. Occasionally we find even more targets to shoot.

Lots of volume in super long range shooting means the hunter can learn a great deal in a relatively short period of time. He learns about super long range wind doping, range estimation, trajectory of the cartridge he shoots, mirage in the scope and dealing with it, plus a lot more. The key to improvement in anything is repetition, and there's lots of repetitive shooting where Cassidy and I concentrate our chucking.

One special bonus of super long range shooting is that the rifleman often gets several tries at the same chuck. When a bullet strikes the ground next to a chuck, he's less likely to be spooked if that projectile has traveled five hundred yards as opposed to two hundred. At two hundred yards the report of a hot centerfire is still plenty loud, but the volume of the cartridge report at five hundred yards is considerably diminished. This means the chuck isn't as likely to associate the bullet's striking close by with the distant noise, at least at first.

Many times the chuck being tried at five hundred yards becomes confused rather than spooked. This means a second shot is very possible, and if the man behind the rifle knows what he's doing, he's going to come much closer with that second bullet because his buddy is going to tell him where the first shot struck. Chucks at an extra long distance might permit several shots before they take refuge subsurface. Once they go underground they're often peaking up again, usually with less underground time involved than when ranges are considerably shorter. When fired at the second time they come above ground, many become even more confused. A fair percentage of them leave the burrow and search for another safer one. Some of these leave with dispatch, but many take their good old time, so several more shots might be possible. Every time the hard working chuck hunter pulls that trigger, he's learning something. He knows how he held before, where his bullet hit, and thus has a better idea where to hold for the next try. He also learns what he has misjudged—and how badly—wind, range, trajectory (though this should be a known entity), etc.

Because of the effect wind has on small bullets at these super long ranges, the 22 centerfires can't match the larger calibers. A 50 grain .224 bullet is not only blown farther off course than a 100 grain .257 bullet—the smaller pill is seldom blown with any degree of consistency. Even if the breeze appears to be a steady one, the first smallish bullet might be blown way off course; the next might be blown far more—or far less. Needed consistency is lacking. This doesn't mean 100 and 120 grain bullets are affected with a high degree of consistency by the wind, but there is no doubt that a shooter can better predict how these larger projectiles are going to be affected by the wind.

Will tomorrow's extra long range cartridges be even larger than today's? I think there's a good chance they will, although rifle rigs even heavier than fifteen pounds might be required to help handle their recoil. There is one small group of riflemen who shoot woodchucks at even farther distances than I'm describing in this chapter. Many of their shots are one thousand yards, and some are far beyond that. One of the popular calibers among this clan is the 30 caliber magnum built on the 338 Winchester Magnum case. Firing something like the 200 grain Sierra Spitzer Boat Tail, this could be a wicked super long range rifle. That bullet has a sectional density of .301, compared to .216 for the 100 grain Sierra .257 Spitzer. The 200 grain can be driven to over 3,000 fps in the 30-338, too, which is not too far behind the hotly loaded 100 grain Sierra in the 25-06!

But how heavy would the rifle have to be for the shooter to handle the recoil with no problem? Some of the folks who fire these guns consistently build tremendously heavy rifles, perhaps weighing thirty-five and forty pounds. These can hardly be lifted from the trunk, let alone be carried in the field. There has to come a time when chuck hunters are going to balk at too much weight. Some balk as soon as they pick up one of Bob Cassidy's fifteen to seventeen pound outfits.

Will some be willing to experiment with even heavier rigs? I believe they will. It makes sense to go all the way up to .308 caliber because so many excellent bullets capable of bench rest accuracy are available. The 7mm caliber can't be sold short either. The 7mm Remington Magnum might be a popular one for the future if suitable bullets for varmints could be obtained. There are a couple of excellent hollow points available in both 7mm and .308, but frankly, I don't like the ballistics hollow points produce. While many are superbly accurate, I feel hollow points slow down in velocity more quickly, thus they don't offer the supreme, flat, long range trajectory everyone shooting at five hundred yards is looking for. Some will dispute my claim, but I'll stick by it. The 100 grain Sierra in .257 and the 120 grain Nosler Solid Base in .264 are tough to beat for five hundred yardish stuff. Some may question even the quick expansion capabilities of the latter bullet, but I can say from my experience of shooting with Bob Cassidy that this Nosler is outstanding on chucks at long range. Bullets we think of as only for big game might perform quite nicely on chucks if driven fast enough. It might pay to experiment with the .270 130 grain Sierra Spitzer Boat Tail for this extra long range work, as well as that company's 160 grain Spitzer Boat Tail in 7mm, their 175 grain Spitzer Boat Tail in the same caliber, then, in .308 caliber, spewing them from a high velocity magnum of some type, Sierra's 165 grain Spitzer Boat Tail, their 190 and 200 grain of the same nomenclature.

Are you ready to graduate to this ultra long varmint shooting game? I urge you to consider it. The added precision required of every facet in this challenge will make you a better rifleman, one who learns and experiences great satisfaction and accomplishment from a very difficult job well done.

Woodchucks with Rimfires

As I took slow steps forward, more and more good chuck country was exposed. I didn't want to move too quickly and have a ground hog see me first. There he was, a bit to the left. I double checked with my binoculars. The quarry was down, feeding avidly. He didn't have a clue I existed.

I stooped down until I could no longer see that pig, then backed my way out the same way I'd walked in. Already my plan for a closer stalk was formulating. Had I been carrying anything but a rimfire that

The author with a chuck and his Remington 5mm rimfire.

day I'd have merely stalked a few more yards to the crest of the little hill, snuggled into the prone position, leveled the crosswires and pulled the trigger.

With rimfire rifles though, close shots are a necessity. My new approach brought me within a hundred yards of that woodchuck, but I had to crawl on my belly for twenty-five yards to get in that position. Even though I tried to stay out of sight, the critter knew I was there—probably spotted my blaze orange cap. He wasn't totally spooked, but he had quit feeding and started ambling towards the safety of his subterranean home. I knew I wouldn't have much time, but I was already firmly in the prone position, though I had no rest for the rimfire rifle's fore-end. I also knew from past experience that this chuck would pause for some seconds at the mound of his hole before disappearing beneath the ground.

My trigger finger was already tightening as the pig made its last few steps toward the freshly made mound of earth. He came off his front feet a bit, standing slightly erect. I squeezed harder as the crosswires bobbed slightly over his chest. The rim cracked. The bullet bowled him over. His tail twitched. His front paws, extending straight in the air, moved for a few seconds in reflex.

I walked to the area, anxious to pick up my prize. The bullet had taken him square in the chest, then passed on through. From the looks of things, the soft lead pill had expanded perfectly. A chuck taken through the chest with a standard rimfire at almost a hundred yards is seldom killed so cleanly with a chest shot, but I wasn't using any ordinary rimfire cartridge.

Instead of a 22 rimfire I was toting an extra light 5mm Remington rim, their Model 591 bolt action with clip feed that is no longer in production. It was topped with a Weaver K856 8X scope with huge objective lens. To get that scope to mount with no problem (due to the big objective lens) I'd chosen a set of "See-Thru" mounts by Weaver. These mounts fit in the grooves of rimfire receivers, but the see-through feature means the scope mounts very high—permitting use of scopes with larger than normal objective lenses on rimfire rifles.

When it comes to rimfire cartridges, the 5mm Remington is in a class by itself. Rather, the 5mm *was* in a class by itself. It's now a has-been, as Remington has eliminated it from the 1982 catalog. This was the only rimfire cartridge ever made on a bottleneck case. Evidently, the price of the ammo was too steep compared to 22 rimfires, thus the demise of a good cartridge for short range woodchuck work.

The standard 22 rim is definitely borderline for animals the size of chucks. Beyond fifty yards only head shots or shots that sever the vertebrae are quick killers. Hit elsewhere, even solidly in the chest, chucks are going to escape into their burrows.

Target type 22 Long Rifle shells have a velocity of about 1,150 fps with a forty grain bullet. Resulting muzzle energy with those ballistics is 117 foot pounds—not much. A minimum of one thousand foot pounds of striking energy has long been the minimum for big game animals the size of white-tailed deer, many of which will only average a hundred pounds. If a woodchuck averages ten pounds (most will be less), we might extrapolate to assume we need a minimum of a hundred foot pounds to effectively kill *Marmota*. A standard velocity 22 rimfire is below those minimum hundred foot pounds almost as soon as it leaves the muzzle.

The so-called "high velocity" 22 Long Rifle cartridge has velocity stepped up to around 1,250 to 1,280 fps, a muzzle energy of 140 foot pounds, which is not all that much of an increase. Today's recently introduced "hyper velocity" 22 Long Rifles spit out 33 and 36 grain pills at around 1,500 and 1,400 fps respectively. Still, their bullet energy is only a bit over 150 foot pounds, less than one hundred foot pounds at one hundred yards. Actually, at one hundred yards, there's no difference between a 40 grain standard velocity Long Rifle (85 pounds) and Remington's "Yellow Jacket" (also 85 foot pounds).

In contrast, the 5mm was a real hummer. It's little 38 grain hollow point zipped along at 2,100 fps. It's muzzle velocity was 372 foot pounds. At a hundred yards that cartridge still had 217 foot pounds of energy. That's why the chuck alluded to at the beginning of this chapter was killed so effectively at almost one hundred yards—bullet energy.

The 22 rimfires have no doubt killed truck loads of woodchucks over the years, but the heyday of this fine little cartridge is drawing to a close around summer hayfields. Today's sportsmen are finding less and less need to "pot vermin." Today's chuck hunter is looking for precision in his shooting, longer range sport, and a wide variety of modern centerfire cartridges can give him what he wants.

This isn't to say that the 22 rim is dead, for it certainly isn't. Nor is my last paragraph a put down for using this little cartridge in summer fields. I simply believe precision shooting and longer shots are the current "state of the art!"

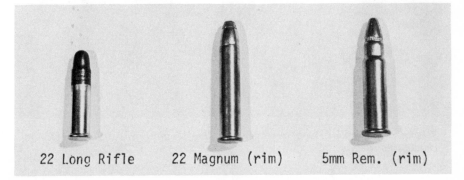

22 Long Rifle   22 Magnum (rim)   5mm Rem. (rim)

33

The 22 rim will continue to be a favorite for serious squirrel hunters, as plinking guns, guns to start youngsters in the shooting sports and more. What are some of the 22 rifles manufactured today that will produce satisfactorily on chucks? Remington's Model 541-S Custom Sporter would be ideal. This is that company's top-of-the-line 22 rim, and it's handsome. A step down the line there's the 581 bolt. In the 22 pump gun realm there's the Model 572A, and for those who like auto-loaders, there's the 552A and the Nylon 66.

For several months I tested the Anschutz Model 64-MS. This one was made specifically for 22 rimfire silhouette shoots, but it's a dandy for chucks if you insist on the 22 rim. Also from Anschutz consider their Model 54 and Model 164, both trim looking and tight shooting sporters.

The Savage Fox FB-1 sporter 22 looks good in a catalog, but I've yet to see one first hand, or know anyone else who has. Browning has several 22 possibilities, their BAR (auto-loader), the BPR (a pump), the BL-22 (a lever) and the regular 22 Automatic. From U.S. Repeating Arms there's only the 9422 lever action. From Marlin there are several different variations of the 39 lever, the 990 and 995 auto-loaders, plus the 780 and 781 bolt guns. H & R has a new 5200 rimfire intended

Relatively short range shots, often from the kneeling position, are called for in hunting chucks with rimfires.

34

for serious target work, plus two bolts, the 750 and 864. From Ruger there's the 10/22 auto-loader.

The 22 Magnum rimfire hasn't been mentioned so far. I have little experience with this one. Produced by both Winchester and CCI, this cartridge is certainly a cut far above any other 22 rim. Velocity with 40 grain bullet is a whopping two thousand foot pounds and bullet energy is 355 foot pounds at the muzzle, 170 foot pounds at one hundred yards. So—it'll do the job on a chuck to that reasonable range.

The following rifles come in 22 Mag: the Browning BPR, the Harrington and Richardson 700 auto-loader, the Marlin 782 bolt, Marlin 640K Chuckster bolt, Sako 78 bolt, Savage 65-M.

Handgunning Woodchucks

I had spotted the chuck from almost two hundred yards away. Normally I'd have settled into a shooting position, placed the rifle on the rest attached to my belt, and steadied the crosswires on the target. However, I didn't have a chuck rifle slung over my shoulder; a handgun was strapped to my hip. When handguns are involved in chuck hunting it becomes a short range contest, not a long range game.

After backing out of sight I took to the woods, hurrying at first, then slowing down and watching where I walked to avoid making too much noise. The chuck was gorging on succulent alfalfa only twenty-five yards out from the woods' edge. Seconds after I spotted him feeding from my position in the woods, the chuck sat up on his haunches. At first I figured he came up from eating to look around and make certain the coast was still clear, but then he quickly came back down on his forelegs, every muscle in his body tense and alert. He'd either spotted me or heard my movements.

Moving painfully slow, I made my way to the woods' edge, eased the scope-sighted Colt Python from its holster, then wedged my left forearm against a stout oak, caught the chuck in the long eye relief scope, stopped breathing as the crosswires settled on the target, then squeezed off the final few ounces on the trigger when his chest area appeared centered.

The range was only about thirty-five yards. The hollow point bullet struck with a whopping thud, bowling the eight pound rodent over in his tracks. A satisfying stalk; a satisfying shot. I walked over to see how the bullet had performed. The 357 Magnum firing a hollow point bullet with a gas check is an excellent killer.

These days most handgunning for woodchucks isn't done by hunters who have "only" a handgun strapped to their hip. Many summer varminters afield have their chuck rifle slung over a shoulder **and** a

The author with a chuck and a Colt Diamondback 22 rimfire.

handgun holstered on their hip. The latter is used, if time permits, when a chuck is suddenly encountered at short, short range; otherwise the shoulder arm swings into action.

Bob Cassidy and I, when enjoying our extra long range hunting, always have a handgun handy for any short range chucks we might spot. A chuck at eighty yards is no challenge if firing a fifteen pound 25/06 with 15X Unertl Ultra Varmint scope from a solid rest. This is when Bob's XP-100 221 Remington Fireball sees duty.

Getting close shots is always a part of handgunning for chucks, as is honing stalking techniques. Most important to consistent scoring with this type of weapon is practice, practice, practice. Effective handgun shooting requires a great deal of hard work at the range, and that work must be repetitive, week after week after week. Most sportsmen are unwilling to put in the time it requires to become an expert handgunner. Those who do are a cut above those who don't when it comes time to measure group sizes on paper targets.

A few decades ago about the only choices one had who wanted to "handgun some chucks" was the 22 rim, later the 22 rim Magnum and maybe the 357. The 41 and 44 Magnums are a bit too much gun for most, though they can be loaded down in velocity and still remain

Using the top of the MTM "Walking Stick," Sisley levels on a short range chuck with his Colt Diamondback in 22 rim.

effective on short range *Marmotas*. The silhouette shooting crowd has spawned a number of new calibers that are better suited to chucks than the rimfires or the big bores. Long eye relief scopes have meant smaller group sizes compared to adjustable open sights.

Before the silhouetters came along, I liked the 256 Winchester. I had one of these in the Thompson/Center Contender, the single shot handgun that has become extremely popular. The 256 was also available in the Marlin Model 62 lever action rifle. Another very specialized handgun with a closed breech handled the high chamber pressure problem of the 256 Winchester. That was the Ruger "Hawkeye." Top handgun velocities were probably around 2,200 fps with the 75 grain .257 hollow point. One day that Contender of mine made it to the trading block. Sometimes I wish I'd kept it. The 256 Winchester was based on the 357 Magnum handgun case.

The 22 Remington Jet was a second "odd ball" handgun cartridge directed toward the varmint hunter. Another specialized handgun had to be developed specifically for the cartridge. This was the Smith & Wesson Model 53, which had a dual firing pin, a rimfire portion to handle rimfires, a centerfire portion to handle the 22 Jet. Bullet velocities (.223 diameter) were in the same realm as the 22 Rim Magnum. The Jet never gained much notoriety.

The 221 Remington Fireball is some fast stepper though. Designed specifically around the XP-100 handgun, it is capable of 2,700 fps with 45 grain Sierra Spitzers. The XP-100 has a tremendous accuracy reputation. It looks like something out of the space age, rather than something that comes off an Ilion, New York, assembly line. In actuality, it's a bolt action, the action resembling the now defunct Remington 600. The XP-100 recently became available in a new cartridge, the 7mm Remington BR (Bench Rest).

The Second Edition of the Sierra Reloading Manual permits faster velocities in the 22 Jet for modern Thompson Contender single shots. With the 40 grain .223 Sierra Hornet bullet, the max charge of 12 grains of 2400 permits 2,450 fps. The Thompson Contender is also available in 22 Hornet and 22 K Hornet. Velocities similar to those just mentioned for the Jet are possible with the regular Hornet, while maximum velocities with the K Hornet are 2,600 fps with the forty grain Sierra .224, 2,500 fps with the 45 grain .224 Sierra.

Interestingly, the Contender is even available in 222 Remington, the varmint cartridge that made it possible for practically any rifleman to become a superb chuck hunter. As much as the 222 was a success in the rifle realm, it's not all that much in a pistol. Velocities will be dramatically less than in rifles, even if reasonably fast burning powders are used. As of this writing the 221 Remington Fireball, in either a Thompson Contender or the XP-100, appears to be the best varmint handgun cartridge. While others approach or even exceed it in velocity, the 221 is the accuracy winner, hands down. The XP-100 normally produces the best accuracy of all. This is because the bolt action locks up so tight and the base of the cartridge rides against something extra firm.

In other words, if handgunning chucks is what turns you on, the XP-100 Remington Fire Ball, equipped with something like the Burris 5X long eye relief (LER) scope with parallex adjustment should be perfect.

The Remington XP-100 in 221 Remington Fireball. This is the weapon most ideally suited for handgunning woodchucks.

Fancy Weatherby's.

CHAPTER 3

The Varmint Gun

From the Factory

You shouldn't have much of a problem to go out and lay your hands on a fine varmint gun these days. Most any small gun shop usually has several excellent factory made considerations. Big shooting shops in metropolitan areas have racks full of varmint getters. It wasn't always that way. Until the 1950's, rifles weren't produced often in varmint calibers. The choice was big game rigs and little else in most emporiums. A custom varmint rifle from a specialized gunsmith was the typical way to acquire one several decades back. Falling block actions were extremely popular. By 1950 Remington introduced its great 222 Remington in a bolt action rifle. Falling block actions, similar to today's Ruger Number One, fell a bit out of favor with varminters. What actually happened was that the 222 and the many bolt actions that were offered in this fine caliber made varminting more popular and available to thousands. Prior to that, long range varminting was a specialized sport for a specialized few. Sure, there were Model 70 Swifts, some 250/3000s and a few others in the early days, but not all that many—other than the custom made rifles.

With all the guns available today for varmint hunting, the prospective buyer's problem is one of making the proper selection. The only way is through careful study. In a subsequent chapter the various varmint cartridges are covered in depth. This section delves into some of the many different rifles and handguns that can be considered for varmint shooting.

41

REMINGTON

No arms company in recent decades has been more tuned into the needs of today's shooters, and this is particularly true with regard to varmint hunters. Remington has made one corporate decision after another that has kept them at the forefront in the arms business, starting with their introduction of the 222 Remington cartridge. Other banner successes include the 222 Remington Magnum, the 223 Remington, the 22-250 Remington (the old "varminter"), 6mm Remington, the 25—06 Remington, to say nothing of stuff like the Model 700 bolt gun, the no-frills 788, the 760 pump, the 870 pump shotgun and the 1100 autoloading smoothbore.

These days Remington finds their niche in the heart of the average varmint hunter with their Model 700 Varmint Special. This one sports a twenty-four inch barrel that tapers to about ⅝ of an inch at the muzzle end. Without scope it'll heft near nine pounds. Add a typical varmint scope and the whole deal will spin a scale needle to between 10½ and eleven pounds. That's too heavy for big game, but easing across summer chuck fields or prairie dogs towns isn't akin to climbing the Rockies or Himalayas. The heavy barrel is only of benefit when the man wrapped around the walnut is using a firm rest. Only then can one of these rigs begin to perform to perfection.

The 700 Varmint Special is offered in 222 Remington, 22-250 Remington, 223 Remington, 6mm Remington, 243 Winchester, 25-06 Remington, 7mm-08 Remington and 308 Remington. Which Varmint Special cartridge is for you depends upon both how you hunt and on what other varmint guns and calibers are in your arsenal. While some readers might be thinking about acquiring their first varmint rifle, chances are 99 to 1 it won't be their last varmint rifle. We all do think that first one will be the only rig we'll ever want. But once bitten with the varmint hunting bug, there's no stopping at any one, two or three rifles. Something new always looks good, as does a caliber different from those rifles in one's possession.

The Varmint Special features a Monte Carlo, full cheekpiece, skip-line checkering, black fore-end tip, hinged floor plate, quick release swivels and sling. In addition to this bull barreled job, Remington offers three more Model 700 considerations with standard weight barrels. Their top-of-the-line is the BDL Custom Deluxe. Varmint calibers available are 222 Rem., 22-250 Rem., 6mm Rem., 243 Win., 25-06 Rem., and 270 Win. In the latter a left hand model is also available.

The standard BDL is a step down, but a small step. It comes in the widest range of varmint calibers: 17 Rem., 222 Rem., 22-250 Rem., 6mm Rem., 243 Win., 25-06 Rem., and 270 Win. The ADL follows, available in 222 Rem., 22-250 Rem., 6mm Rem., 243 Win., 25-06 Rem. and 270 Win. The 700 "Classic" is a personal favorite. This one has the clean

Remington Model 788 Bolt Action Rifle with 4X scope and 24-inch barrel. Calibers: 223 Rem. and 22-250 Rem.

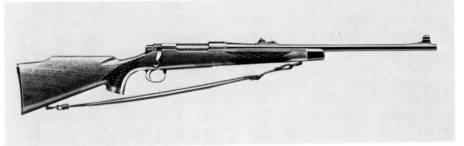

Remington Model 700 BDL Bolt Action Center Fire Rifle.

Remington Model 700 BDL "Varmint Special" *Bolt Action Center Fire Rifle.*

Remington Model 40-XB "Rangemaster" *Bolt Action Center Fire Target Rifle.*

lines many of us prefer in a rifle, a satin wood finish, and more. The "Classic" is available in 22-250, 6mm Rem., 243 Win., 257 Roberts, and 270 Win.

The Remington 788 no-frills bolt gun has been another of the company's supreme success stories. The idea behind this gun was to produce something very inexpensive for deer hunters—and that they've done with the little 18½ inch barrel versions in 243 Win., 308 Win., and most lately, with the 7mm-08 Rem. However, their 788 in 223 Rem. and 22-250 with 24-inch barrels have found much favor with experienced riflemen because they shoot well and have good triggers. Recently the 222 Rem. was reintroduced to the 788 line.

The very top of the Remington line, though, especially when it comes to long range chucks, crows and prairie dogs, is their renowned 40-X. These are special order rifles only. The 40-X action is a dandy, with a deserved reputation among the bench rest crowd. In single shot it's available in 222 Rem., 22-250 Rem., 243 Win., 6mm Rem., 25-06 Rem., while in repeaters it's available in 222 Rem., 22-250 Rem., 243 Win., and 6mm Rem. Two weights of barrels can be specified, either a ¾ incher or a ⅞ incher. The former will result in a rifle that totes about 9¼ pounds, the latter about 11¼ pounds. Two ounce triggers are available, but the standard trigger is adjustable for light, crisp pulls. The 40-X Remington is perhaps the best varmint rifle available today without going the custom gun route. Of course this 40-X is sort of a custom gun in its own right, since it's a special order item.

The XP-100 is Remington's little bolt gun affixed to a handgun type stock. It can add plenty of challenge to anyone's varmint hunting. It's available in the 221 Remington Fire Ball, has a 10½ inch barrel and a stock of DuPont "Zytel" nylon. It spits out 50 grain soft points with the amazing velocity of 2,650 fps, unheard of in a handgun. Recently Remington made the XP–100 available in 7mm Remington BR (Bench Rest).

Finally from Remington, don't sell its current pump gun short, the Model Six. Its predecessor, the Model 760, was a winner from the bench, many of these rifles capable of minute of angle accuracy. A friend had a 760 in 222 Remington, and it was a gem. Today's Model Six in 6mm Remington or 243 Winchester will be a winner in both the summer hay fields and the whitetail woods.

RUGER

While Remington has been moving to the forefront of the firearms industry since 1950 or so, Sturm, Ruger & Co. has been coming on like gangbusters. Ruger doesn't make committee decisions. Bill Ruger, the driving force behind this company makes them, and Bill's almost never wrong. His success with regard to items like single action revolvers, auto-loading pistols, falling block actions in the Number One and Number Three Rugers, the Mini-14, and Red Label shotguns has made history. If Bill Ruger had enjoyed the huge Remington plant and the dollar backing of that corporate conglomerate, there's no telling how much more of an impact he would have made on the firearms industry. There's no question he has left an indelible mark, and Ruger will continue to do so.

Ruger has several outstanding offerings for varmint hunters. Heading his list is the Model 77 Varmint model bolt rifle, the one with 24 inch heavy barrel, similar to Remington's 700 Varmint Special. This one is currently available in 22-250, 220 Swift, 243 Win., 6mm Rem., and 25-06 Rem. Like the Remington counterpart, it's fitted with target blocks for target type scopes, and drilled and tapped for receiver mounted scopes. Of late, this latter type of scope set up is becoming more favored. Ruger one inch scope rings and bases are supplied with the rifle, and they are excellent. The trigger is adjustable.

The Ruger Number One Single Shot also comes in a heavy barrel version. It's available in the same calibers as the Model 77 Varmint, but will weigh a pound less overall. The Number One offers traditionalism that was a part of varminting back in the 1920's, 30's and 40's, but the rifle is made of all modern materials, with excellent trigger—and it's a shooter. I don't especially like it as a "sandbag" gun because the fore-end doesn't have a "wide flat" for super stability.

The Number One is available in standard weight versions, as is the 77 bolt job. The calibers already alluded to are offered, with the exception of the 25-06. Weight is much trimmed. I particularly favor the 77. It comes with 22 inch barrel, except 24 inch for the Swift. Some odd calibers have been offered at various times during the past.

The Ruger Number Three single shot falling block is also a possibility for varmint hunters, as it's offered in 22 Hornet and 223 Remington. This is sort of a no-frills single shot, but it's a shooter through and through. The price is right, but attractive price has always been a special bonus of Ruger guns.

When it comes to handguns for varmint hunting, Bill Ruger comes through again. His Security-Six is of rather recent vintage and is available with adjustable sights. In 357 Magnum there's plenty of punch for little critters like chucks. The huge Ruger Redhawk is very tough to find in 44 Magnum, but it's a terror once it strikes anything. It's in the single action realm that Ruger offers so much value—the Convertible Blackhawk (45 Colt or 45 ACP), the Blackhawk and the Super Blackhawk, the latter two in 357 and 41 Mag. and 44 Mag. respectively.

WINCHESTER (U.S. REPEATING ARMS COMPANY)

The famous New Haven plant was sold by Winchester to U.S. Repeating Arms Company. How long the Winchester name will be retained is a matter of conjecture. No matter, though, because New Haven still offers several rifle possibilities for the varmint hunter. Heading the list is the Model 70 XTR Varmint, the company's heavy barrel counterpart to the Remington 700 and Ruger 77. These heavy barrels are 24 inches long, the stocks have Monte Carlos with cheekpiece and

are drilled and tapped for scope mounting. This one is currently only available in 22-250 and 243, but both are excellent chuck getters.

The only way to get a currently produced 264 Winchester Magnum, an outstanding long range varmint cartridge (except from Alpine), is in the Model 70 XTR Sporter Magnum. This isn't a bull barrel version, but at least it's a 264. The Model 70 Westerner comes in 243 and 270, good considerations. The Model 70 XTR Featherweights are selling like hotcakes. Varmint caliber considerations are 243, 257 Roberts and 270. This one has classic lines, weighs only 6¾ pounds without scope (so does the standard Ruger 77), Schnabel fore-end, and satin finish. All Model 70's currently being built are epoxy bedded, and that should improve accuracy considerably if done properly.

SAVAGE

Savage Arms discontinued the heavy barrel version of their 110 bolt gun, called the 112V. I have one in 25-06 and 220 Swift. Both are excellent chuck guns when triggers are adjusted by a master gunsmith. Trigger replacement would be even better. When the 112V, a single shot, was discontinued, it was replaced by the 112R, a repeater. Both had ⅝ inch barrels. Now only standard barrel versions of the company's 110 bolt gun are left. The 110-C is available in 243 Winchester, 22-250, and 270 with 22 inch barrel, 25-06 in 24 inch barrel. This one features a detachable clip magazine.

For the economy minded, there's the Savage 340, available in 22 Hornet, 222 Rem., and 223 Rem. It also has a clip. The same company produces the Stevens Model 110-E—in 243 Win. While lever guns aren't popular with most varmint hunters, the Savage 99-C is available in 243 Win., the 99-A in 243 and 250/3000 (250 Savage), and the 99-E in 243. The 99-C is the dressed up and clip version, the 99-E the no-frills, and the 99-A the straight stock with no pistol grip model.

SAKO

These Finnish made guns were the rage for several years after their introduction. Though their popularity has waned a bit, Sakos still have their champions. They do have a heavy barrel version that weighs from 8¼ to 8½ pounds. It comes in 222 and 223 Rem., 220 Swift, 22-250, 243 Win. and 25-06. The Sako Standard Sporter has the standard diameter barrel, a 23-incher that comes in 222, 223 and 243, a 24-incher in 17 Rem., 22-250, 220 Swift, 25-06 and 270. There are several other Sako models with varying frill dressings, all spin offs of the Standard Sporter. One that isn't is the Model 78. This one comes in 22 Hornet.

PARKER-HALE

These rifles are imported from England and are attractively priced. A Varmint model is available—the 1200V. This one comes without sights in 22-250, 243, 6mm Rem., and 25-06. The standard barrel 1200 comes in all these calibers, plus 270 Win. The Parker-Hale features hand checkered walnut, rose wood pistol grip and fore-end caps, plus rubber recoil pad fitted with white spacers.

WEATHERBY

Roy Weatherby is currently offering a wide range of varmint rifle possibilities, and they fall into two categories, his Mark V bolt gun that takes cartridges of his own design with belted cases, plus his Vanguard line which is available in popular calibers. Let's look at the Mark V possibilities first.

Heading the list is his 224 Weatherby, closely followed by his 240 Weatherby Magnum. Mark V's have a lot of luster, extra high cheekpieces on their Monte Carlos, and the wood is usually fancy. The 257 Weatherby might be considered as a varmint rig as well.

Varmint caliber considerations in the Vanguard line are the 243, 25-06 and 270. I have been mentioning the 270 a lot in standard weight bolt rifles—as a varmint possibility. It is just that—a possibility. This is an excellent cartridge for big game, fine for woodchucks, but there's plenty of recoil in a 270 eight pound rifle and scope rig, even with 100 or 110 grain bullets, but this is also true of standard weight 25-06 bolt guns. However, I've carried the 270 as a possible varmint cartridge in the chapter that covers them all. The 270 is at its varmint best in a heavy barreled rifle. None are currently available from the factories (with the exception of the Tikka Model 65 which follows), but the 270 should not be sold short as a custom heavy weight for long range varminting.

TIKKA

This company has several rifle possibilities, though I haven't had one in hand for inspection. It's doubtful Tikkas will be on the average gunshop shelf, but your dealer might order one for you. The heavy barrel version is dubbed the Model 65. The bull barrel is only 22 inches, but the rig without scope is supposed to weigh 9½ pounds. It comes in 25-06 and 270 for varmint consideration. The fore-end is stippled and there's a pistol grip swell. Designed for ISU shooting, this one'll make a fine summer chuck gun.

The Tikka Model 55 Standard Sporter comes in 17 Rem., 222 Rem., 22-250 and 243. The Model 55 Sporter is a 23 inch heavy barrel job that comes in 222, 22-250 and 243. There's also a regular barrel weight version of the Model 64. Varminters will want to look at the 25-06 in this one.

COLT

Colt Sauer rifles are imported from Europe and more expensive than the varmint possibilities covered thus far. Their Short Action Colt Sauer is available in 22-250, and 243. The standard length Colt Sauer comes in 25-06 and 270 for varmint consideration. These are handsome pieces, but there are no true "heavy" barrel varmint possibilities from Colt.

Lots of Colt handgun possibilities are available, if you consider their 357 Magnum and bigger guns. The 22 rimfire is fine, but ranges must be necessarily short. The best of the Colt bunch for this is the Diamondback. The Python is the best bet for chucking in the centerfire Colt line. In years past I personally accounted for a number of chucks with my Python, which has since been put on the trading block for some other varmint hunting ordnance.

INTERARMS

Interarms has entered the centerfire rifle market in a big way, but to date they have not offered any heavy barrel versions. They are long on models available in standard weight barrels though. The Mark X Viscount might be called their no-frills model, but it's still handsome. Chuck specialists will want to look at this one in 22-250, 243, 25-06 and 270. The Mark X is the line's biggest seller. Same varmint caliber choices as for the Viscount. The top of the Mark X line is the Cavalier—also the same varmint cartridge choices. There are two Mannlicher styles in the Mark X, yet I wouldn't favor these for varminting over the three covered so far. They are the Mark X Carbine in 270 and the Mark X Continental in 243 or 270. Both of these have twenty inch barrels and are better suited to big game work.

BROWNING

It's a mystery why the new Browning, the Lightning Bolt, comes only in 25-06 and 270 for varmint consideration. Bet the company would sell plenty of stuff like 243's and 6mm's if they were offered. Even a 22-250 would be a good seller in the Lightning Bolt. This one has a free floating barrel (makes it easy to stock them), and anti-warp forearm design that's successful—an inlay of structural aluminum in the channel under the barrel, plus an adjustable trigger.

The Browning 78 is evidently this firm's answer to the Ruger Number One. This falling block single shot action comes in 22-250, 6mm Rem., and 25-06 for varmint consideration. The barrel on the 78 isn't a heavy one, but it is 26 inches long. The hammer is exposed—unlike the Ruger Number One. Scope rings and bases are provided from Browning.

SMITH & WESSON

S & W imports a rifle from Japan they call the 1500. Varminters will find a 22 inch heavy barrel version of the 1500, available in 222, 223 and 22-250. The standard weight 1500 comes in 243, 25-06 and 270 for varmint shooting. The barrel is 22 inches, the receiver is drilled and tapped and sports a hinged floor plate. The deluxe version offers skip-line hand checkering, an engine turned bolt, and a Monte Carlo type stock.

Like Colt, S & W offers a wide variety of handguns that might be considered for varminting. Also like Colt, they offer no true small diameter varmint calibers—the standard 22 rims, the 38 and 357 Mag., plus the 9mm, 41 and 44 Mags., finally the 45's. Of the bunch, the new N frame Model 27 would be the best for varminting—in 357 Mag. I gave up on that gun many years ago. Too much kick for me, but then everyone isn't as big a pussycat as I am when it comes to recoil.

MANNLICHER

Mannlicher is another import with a fine variety of rifles. The good news is they have heavy barrel varmint models—in 222 Rem., 222 Rem. Mag., 223 Rem., 22-250, and 243 Win. The price is steeper than for a Remington or Ruger Heavy Barrel, but the Mannlicher is a fine looking rifle. Their other models don't come in varmint calibers.

KLEINGUENTHERS

Kleinguenther in Texas imports this one—and these are tack drivers—guaranteed to shoot small groups, this even though they come only in standard weight barrel versions. Made in Germany, they're drilled and tapped. Varmint calibers available include 243, 25-06, and 270.

ALPINE

This one is imported from England and comes with a 23 inch standard weight barrel. For the varmint minded there's the 22-250, 243

Win., and 264 Win. Mag. (the only place this writer knows where you can get a 264 other than through U.S. Repeating Arms). The Alpine is a fine looking rifle, and the price tag won't scare you off.

TRADEWINDS

The Husky Model 5000 is the moniker for this import. A racy looker, it comes in 22-250, 243 and 270 for varmint shooting. Lots of white spacers, adjustable trigger and clip.

BSA

Another standard weight barrel centerfire imported from England— the varmint shooter will want to consider their 222 Rem., 22-250 Varminter, 243 and 270 Winchesters. This one has a Monte Carlo and rollover, skip line checkering, high gloss finish, and adjustable trigger.

SHILEN

Finally, there's the Shilen. This one moves more into the custom gun category, which makes the transition to the next chapter easy. The Shilen has a special extra stiff action, and the barrels are legendary for their accuracy. The DGA Benchrest Model comes in 22-250 and fiberglass stock—choice of thumbhole or classic. It can be weighted to the customer's specs. This is a sweet shooter, but as mentioned, the Shilen is truly a custom varmint rig.

The Custom Built Long Range Rifle

Not too long ago, custom built varmint rifles were almost a necessity. There simply weren't that many suitable chuck pieces available from the factories. That period also marked an age when taking the time to tinker with firearms was more popular. Today most of us are finding less and less time for tinkering because so much of our days and evenings must be devoted to making a living. Fortunately for us varmint hunters, there is a tremendous variety of excellent long range factory woodchuck rifles available today.

Of course there are still those who build their own these days, or have them built. One reason for doing this is to obtain a rifle that shoots significantly smaller groups than rifles built on factory assembly lines. It should be pointed out that rifles built on today's assembly lines are capable of accuracy which exceeds the assembly line rifles of yesteryear. A high percentage of modern bolt action rifles of as-

Bob Cassidy and five of his current custom-built varmint rifles—from left to right: a 22-250, 6mm Rem., 6mm-284, 25-06 and 6.5-06.

sembly line vintage are capable of 1½ minute of angle accuracy, especially those produced by certain manufacturers.

A second reason for building a custom made rifle is for extra long range shooting, as covered earlier. When shots of four or five hundred and even longer ranges are involved, a rifle that shoots extra tight groups, less than a minute of an angle preferable, one that sits the sand bags or rests better than factory rifles for added stability, and one that weighs enough to make recoil negligible, has definite merit.

Bob Cassidy, mentioned often in this book, has built scores of his own custom varmint rifles over the years. He's proof that if you're a good home tinkerer and have the desire to produce an outstandingly accurate varmint rifle, it can be done. Of course there may be readers who want a genuine custom rifle for woodchucks or other varmints, yet they want a fine custom maker to do it for them. Only by learning some of the many factors that go into a fine custom chuck piece will anyone be able to talk intelligently about the subject. I've picked Bob Cassidy's brain on several occasions about building custom long range rifles. Here are some of the things I've learned.

The first decisions for the person who wants a custom job are caliber and cartridge. Which one will best suit the shooting he has in mind? The main question is, "How long will the ranges be?" A secondary one is, "How will wind affect the bullet at that range on the average hunting day?" It's Cassidy's view that the highest velocity is extremely important. For the extra long range work he and I concentrate on, high velocity means flat trajectory. The ballistic coefficient of the bullet is equally important. Only a bullet with a high ballistic coefficient will efficiently maintain velocity and subsequent flat trajectory. Consequently, the long range buff should choose not only his caliber and cartridge before moving further, he should also choose the specific bullet he wants to use for that work.

Bob's feeling is that a fine custom built rifle should have at least one minute of angle capabilities, preferably ¾ minute, though I know some of his custom rigs are capable of better than that. He's adamant about how his groups look. A one inch group that's roundish is far better than a one inch group that strings the holes vertically, horizontally or diagonally.

According to Bob, "Long range chuck shooting is a matter of accumulated guess work." Better ballistic coefficients in longer and larger diameter bullets have lead him to bigger cases, bigger calibers and heavier chuck outfits. He once thought the 220 Swift was the ultimate because the trajectory was so flat, but he came to know the little 50 and 55 grain .224 bullets could be blown many feet off track at five hundred yards, and that the smaller the bullet, the less predictable wind drift would be. In a steady breeze, a 100 grain Sierra spit fast from a 25-06, might drift almost three feet at 550 yards, but the wind drift will be reasonably consistent from shot to shot. Not so with bullets of half that weight.

Most of the custom rifles Bob has made over the years have been traded off or sold outright. Five of those in his current arsenal are— a 244 Rem., a 6mm-284, a 22-250, a 25-06 and a 6.5 mm-06. Both these latter guns are chambered for the 270 Winchester rather than the 30-06 case. These cases are very similar to both the eye and the micrometer, but 270 cases are made to withstand chamber pressures of 54,000 psi, while 30-06 cases must regularly stand up to only 50,000 psi. From this Bob assumes 270 cases must be made inherently stronger.

At this point in time Bob feels the ultimate long range (four to six hundred) chuck rifle is the 25-06 zipping out a 100 grain bullet at max velocity or 6.5mm-06 zipping out a 120 grain bullet at max velocity. I tend to agree with him. In Bob's guns we're talking about tremendous weight, probably over fifteen pounds. These are not guns for carrying. Bigger calibers and heavier bullets mean recoil is going to become a factor in the precision you're trying to attain.

Once the decision of cartridge in conjunction with what you want it to do from a velocity, range, accuracy and windbucking standpoint has been made, the next task should be barrel selection. The barrel for your custom chuck gun is no place to skimp on shekels. The best costs only a little more than the run-of-the-mill. Cassidy has enjoyed his best barrel luck with those from two manufacturers, Hart and Shilen. He feels the Douglas Premium Grade barrels are a very close second. Naturally Bob hasn't had the benefit of using barrels from every barrel maker there is.

The larger the cartridge selected, the heavier the barrel one should choose. Most of Bob's latest rifles sport barrels of one or 1⅛ inch diameter, and they don't taper, either. Heavy barrels like this have a couple of important advantages. They minimize recoil, pretty much eliminating the need to add lead weight to the gun stock. Heavy barrels also tend to shoot more accurately. This is probably because the vibration waves set up upon firing are more consistent with heavier barrels. These barrels have more stability on the rest or sand bags, another factor that contributes to better accuracy. Bob also likes long barrels. They add extra weight, and a 26, 27 or 28 inch barrel gives a tad more velocity, always something to be strived for in the long range game where flat trajectory is so beneficial. The disadvantage of a one or 1⅛ inch barrel is weight for carrying. There's no way any chuck hunter is going to carry a gun of fifteen or more pounds very far.

The barrel's twist is extremely important. Twist determines bullet stability. Too much or too little barrel twist results in a bullet that exits the muzzle spinning improperly. This is another reason for deciding upon what bullet you want to shoot before you make the decision of which barrel to buy. Tell your barrel maker what cartridge and bullet you've decided upon. Only then will he be able to provide the barrel with the optimal twist.

Next comes the selection of a good gunsmith. A great gun fixer is not the type to seek out. Try to find a knowledgeable gunsmith who is also a bench rest or chuck shooter. He'll know all the intricacies and secrets that add up to a rifle capable of producing small groups. The barrel, as it comes from the manufacturer, should next be cut off, a portion from both ends. This eliminates the slight imperfections that come at these points in the barrel making.

The knowledgeable gunsmith then determines the direction of the barrel's grain structure. The bullet's flight path must be with, not against the grain structure. The muzzle of the barrel must be crowned perfectly square. Proper crowning insures the bullet won't tip to one side when it exits the muzzle. If the muzzle is uncrowned or crowned incorrectly, gas can escape unevenly just as the bullet is leaving the muzzle. This will cause bullet tipping and large groups.

The barrel is then chambered for the cartridge you've chosen. This is precision work. Prevail only upon gunsmiths who have considerable experience in this field. Putting the chamber in the exact center of the barrel is of extreme importance, but doing so isn't all that easy. The

Perfect muzzle crowning is an integral part of the accurate varmint rifle.

sophistication of the gunsmith's machining equipment now becomes a factor, as well as his experience, care and attention to detail.

Now you'll need to put the threads on the barrel, getting it ready for a precision fit to the action. Here the fit must be perfect. Again, that perfection is not always easy to achieve. Since nothing has been said so far about action choice, let's discuss that issue next.

Action choices are not as important as barrel choices. Here one can perhaps skimp on cost and experience little or no sacrifice in varmint accuracy. Cassidy told me it is relatively easy to weld a plate in many of the Remington actions—a plate in the magazine area that will greatly stiffen the action. He went on to say that stiffening most other actions by welding in a plate bordered on being extremely difficult to next to impossible. A stiffer action generally results in better accuracy.

Take my experience with two Savage heavy barrel 25-06's. One was their single shot 112V, plenty stiff because instead of a magazine this area had been forged solid with the receiver. The other Savage was a 112R, a repeater with the typical box magazine of the standard bolt action. The 112V was a better shooter. Both sported heavy barrels, ⅝ inch diameter at the muzzle end.

The Remington actions Cassidy told me to suggest for easy welding of the magazine area with a stiffening plate are 700's, 721's, 722's and XP-100's. The Remington 40-X is already a single shot (a repeater version is available.) Bob's favorite actions are the Pre-64 Model 70 Winchesters and the Model 98 Mausers, though that choice is more from an esthetics point of view rather than one of increased accuracy.

Bob has also used Argentine Mausers, Japanese Mausers, Post-64 Model 70 Winchesters, and a few others. When glass bedded properly to the stock, and coupled with the best in a heavy weight barrel, all these actions are capable of minute of angle accuracy and less.

Next comes the custom stock. Bob Cassidy has been whittling on walnut for almost thirty years. Using his tips and following instructions from other sources, you can do a creditable bedding and stocking job yourself. If you're not the tinkering kind, there are a number of custom gunsmiths who can do the wood work for you. Some gunsmiths specialize in both the metal work and wood work involved in producing tack holers, while others specialize in one or the other. Consequently, you may have to use one gunsmith to do your barrel and action work; then another smith to build the near perfect fitting stock.

Many aspects of the stock are esthetic rather than meaningful with regard to reducing group size. Esthetics can mean different likes and dislikes for different people. Let's try to eliminate the esthetic parts of good gun stock building and concentrate on those that are important to accuracy. Of prime importance to any gun that is going to be shot off a rest or off sand bags is a wide, flat fore-end. A fore-end on a big game rifle, which is typically held in the hand while firing, is naturally totally different than one suggested for serious shooting from the solid rest. This flat bottom of the fore-end should not be checkered either. Smoothness in this area results in straight line recoil, an aid to producing small groups. Checkering will tend to bind and prevent the rifle from coming staright back upon firing.

Cassidy suggests very high combs for the scope sighted long range chuck rifle, but he doesn't like Monte Carlos. Note the high, straight comb in the photo of his 25-06. This high, straight comb style rides high on the shoulder, thus recoil comes straight back into the shoulder. Bob claims a stock with a Monte Carlo fits the face okay, but the butt stock's position on the shoulder has to be lower. When the position is lower, recoil tends to be less than straight back, resulting in slight upward movement of the stock—thus into the sensitive face area where we have no natural padding.

Glass bedding, done properly, can be a key to today's custom chuck rifle when you expect to shoot small groups. One place to buy glass bedding kits is Bob Brownell, Main and Third, Montezuma, Iowa 50171.

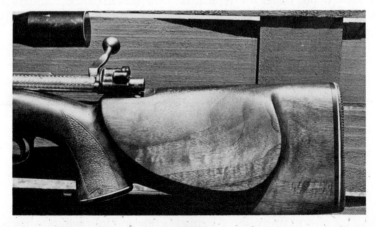

Note high comb on Cassidy's custom stock. The high comb means less recoil, especially to the face area, and presents the perfect position for the eye to view through the scope.

56

Complete instructions accompany these kits, so there's no need to expound upon the how-to here. Suffice to say the bedding at the recoil lug (where the front screw goes into the receiver) is one key area. It must be perfect. Another key area to bed perfectly is at the rear of the action's tang. The use of fiberglass, after enough wood has been gouged out in these two areas will significantly improve the accuracy of the average rifle.

Many stock makers, Cassidy included, bed the rear two inches of the barrel channel as well (just in front of action and recoil lug area). Glass bedding here tends to give the barrel more stability—and probably permits the barrel to vibrate with more consistency. Cassidy suggests glassing three and a half inches, maybe a little bit further out the barrel channel if using an extremely heavy barrel. This additional bedding area seems to give that extra heavy barrel a bit more stability and support.

If the custom gun won't shoot satisfactorily after all the above has been carefully done, it may pay to glass the very end of the barrel channel. A bit of pressure on the barrel here can improve accuracy to some degree, but most gunsmiths suggest doing this only after firing unacceptable groups without tip-of-fore-end pressure. Occasionally it'll pay to glass bed the entire barrel channel. This will put pressure under the barrel, and support and stabilize it for the full length.

The action must sit evenly in the stock. If it binds into a twist when the action screws are drawn up tight, it's a sure fire bet that accuracy is going to be sacrificed, probably to a significant degree. Again, glass bedding tends to minimize action twist, if enough wood has been gouged out before coating and filling with the liquid fiberglass. One reason for suggesting welding a plate in the Remington actions is to minimize the possibility of action twist. Actions with plenty of beef, single shot models, and those with welded plates in the magazine area, will naturally tend to twist less under screwdriver pressure as the action screws are drawn tight.

Cassidy says one thing to look for if accuracy is less than expected in your finished custom rig are the holes the screws fit up through. If there are any marks along the sides of the screw holes, it indicates binding and twist. A possible solution is merely to drill out these holes oversize to eliminate the screws from touching. You might want to glass bed the sides of the gun stock as well, though these areas aren't generally as critical as the recoil lug area and the rear of the tang.

The Redfield Jr. one piece mount can act as an action stiffener, as can a one piece block that goes across the top of the action—to which the target scope mounts are attached—note photo.

Checkering the pistol grip area does help to keep the gun from slipping during recoil. Checkering of the sides of the fore-end are strictly cosmetic. If you have a stock maker checker your walnut, don't forget—tell him not to checker the wide, flat bottom of your fore-end. Stippling is also very good. It can be done with relatively inexpensive tools, and it can be done much quicker (thus with less expense) than hand checkering. I frankly, like the no-slip feel of stippling better than even the best checkering.

A top trigger contributes to anyone's ability to fire small groups on paper, as well as to produce the proper let-off in the summer chuck field. Of today's custom triggers, Cassidy claims the Canjar is best. The Timney is less expensive but very good. I find Canjars in very short supply, and so do most gunsmiths I talk with.

The main factor in a trigger is crispness, no creep. Bob sets his triggers for about a one pound let off. The Remington 40-X has a high quality trigger, but, to my knowledge, it isn't adaptable to many, if any, other actions. It has excellent adjustment features. Many of the triggers on modern day bolt actions have adjustable triggers, but they're very difficult to fine tune for the very best in precision accuracy work. Often the best solution is to scrap the trigger your action came with and buy a Canjar or a Timney.

When it comes to scopes, Cassidy still prefers the larger, heavier, target type, especially those from the Pittsburgh based firm, John Unertl. As far as Bob is concerned, this company's Ultra Varmint scope, with its two inch objective lens and outstanding inside optics, is the ultimate scope for the true, long range custom built chuck rifle.

He does admit that standard scopes have come a long way within the last few years. Serious bench rest shooters and silhouette shooters demanded better, lighter, standard scopes because their rifles had to meet specific weight maximums. Serious chuck hunters who use these

This scope base bridges the top of the action, adding strength and reducing the possibility of action twist when tightened into the stock.

modern scopes that attach to standard bases instead of target blocks have reaped the benefits.

Because firms like Remington, Ruger, Sako and a few others produce such outstanding varmint rifles today, there's less and less need for custom built rifles, especially when we're talking about shooting chucks and other varmints at ranges of 200 to 350 yards, yardages the vast, vast majority of today's woodchucks are shot at. However, for those interested in graduating to longer ranges, a step up in equipment is in order. The answer is a custom built rifle.

CUSTOM STOCK MAKERS

Brown Precision, P.O. Box 270W, Los Molinos, CA 96055—916-384-2506. They specialize in fiberglass stocks.

Reinhart Fajen, Box 338, Warsaw, MO 65355—314-438-5111

Paul Jaeger, 211 Leedom St., Jenkintown, PA 19046—215-884-6920

Jim Peightal, #6 8th St., Ernest PA 15739—412-349-5216

Six Enterprises, 6564 Hidden Creek Dr., San Jose, CA 95120—408-268-8296. They also specialize in fiberglass.

Brent Umberger, Sportsman's Haven, R.D. #4, Cambridge OH 43725

CUSTOM BARREL MAKERS

Christy Gun Works, 875 57th St., Sacramento, CA 95819

Douglas Barrels, 5504 Big Tyler Rd., Charleston, WV 25312

Federal Firearms, Box 145, Oakdale, PA 15071

Hart Rifle Barrels, R.D. #2, Lafayette, NY 13084

David Huntington, RFD #1, Box 23, Heber City, UT 84032

Nu-Line Guns, 1053 Caulkshill Rd., Harvester, MO 63303

Ed Shilen Rifles, 205 Metropark Blvd. Ennis, TX 75119

Titus Barrels, RFD #1, Box 23, Heber City, UT 84032

One Specialized Varmint Rifle

After fooling with scores of different rifles for more than two decades, I began thinking more and more about one in the custom realm that more ideally suited extra long range shooting. A custom rifle of some

The 40-XB Remington in 25-06 with blaze orange Six Enterprises Shilen Classic Fiberglass stock.

sort eventually begins filtering its way into many of our daydreams, our conversations with fellow gun cranks, our correspondence with sportsmen friends based in distant places. No wonder I wasn't immune from such afflictions.

Don't get the impression that I'm giving up on factory rifles, for I'm not. Many (not all) of today's factory rifles are perfectly suited to the chuck hunting we've come to know in recent years—the two to four hundred yard shot. One factor that swayed me toward a specialty rig for super long range was recoil in 25-06 class cartridges, plus more weight so the rifle would sit on the rest with the stability hardly to budge the crosswires as they leveled on a chuck at five hundred yards. A factory heavy barrel 25-06 recoils a little, plus I could see that eleven pounds total weight wasn't quite enough for extra steady holds at extreme distances. How to build a better mouse trap?

I was also sold on fiberglass for this gun's stock. Only trouble was, fiberglass was lighter than wood. If I chose this modern material over walnut, it'd mean an even lighter rifle. That wasn't what I was after. Several conversations with Lee Six and his daughter Cindy of Six Enterprises (6564 Hidden Creek Dr., San Jose, CA 95120—Phone 408-268-8296) had the problem solved. Lee said it would be easy to add weight in the form of lead to one of his stocks. So fiberglass it would be instead of walnut.

My original plan was to buy a barrel from Shilen, Hart, or Douglas, one of these premier makers, and purchase some type of action to go with it—then have a gunsmith who knew what he was doing perform the metal work. The more I studied these possibilities, the more muddied those waters became. That's when Dick Dietz of Remington Arms came to the rescue, recommending one of that company's renowned 40-X rifles. The 40-X is offered in the cartridge I wanted: 25-06. I could get a ⅞ inch heavy stainless steel barrel. The trigger was both excellent and adjustable. The 40-X would have all the ingredients that contribute to making one of the finest of varmint rifles and there'd be no hassle of buying barrel, separate action, then having a gunsmith (who I hadn't found yet) do the metal work. It took some doing to get a barreled action from Remington, rather than the completely stocked 40-X, but my being a gun writer no doubt helped. The 40-X barreled action from Remington and the fiberglass stock from Six Enterprises arrived within 24 hours of one another.

During discussions with Lee Six we decided the best stock to add weight to with lead, commensurate with easy fit to the 40-X barreled action, would be his Shilen Classic. It normally weighs one pound eleven ounces. Lee added around six pounds of lead when I told him I was looking for over fifteen pounds of finished weight. I liked the stock's lines in Lee's catalog, and liked these lines even more when I saw the stock fresh out of the box.

Pigmenting or painting? Six, at no extra cost, provides fiberglass stocks to which pigment has been added. A variety of colors are available, but brown or black pigmenting appear to be the most popular among his customers. Other possibilities are dark green, bright blue and red. I didn't ponder long about whether to go for a pigmented stock or have it painted after all the final bedding was completed. I wanted to have mine gaudily dressed, and blaze orange seemed the perfect color choice for a chuck gun. Pigmenting looks far more tra-

The 40-XB fiberglass stock by Six Enterprises—after glass bedding the action area.

61

ditional on a rifle, and this is certainly what I would recommend on a more classic big game rig. My blaze orange 40-X with fiberglass stock is Nick Sisley's Conversation Piece.

There are a number of different 40-X Remingtons from which to choose. The 540-XR is the 22 rim version of the 40-X. The 540-XRJR is designed with younger, smaller shooters in mind—its stock being 1¾ inch shorter. A step up the 22 rim line puts us at the 40-XR. The 40-XBBR comes with the bench-rest shooter in mind, twenty or twenty-four inch barrels chambered for the 22 BR Rem., 222 Rem., 223 Rem., 6 × 47, 6mm BR Rem., and 008 Win. The 40-XC comes in 308 and is designed as a National Match Course Rifle.

Rounding out the 40-X line is the one best suited to chuck shooting of many different types—the 40-XB "Rangemaster," the barreled action I eventually had fitted to the Lee Six weighted fiberglass Shilen Classic stock. This 40-XB comes in many calibers, 222 Rem., 22-250 Rem., 243 Win., 6mm Rem., 25-06 Rem., 7mm Rem. Mag., 308 Win., 30-06, and 30-338. All are single shots, to my mind the only one worth considering if varmint hunting is what you plan on doing with the rig. Repeater versions are available in 222 Rem., 22-250 Rem., 243 Win., 6mm Rem., and 308 Win.

A match type adjustable trigger is provided. Catalog literature claims it can be adjusted from 1½ to 3¼ pounds—and it can be adjusted externally. You can pay extra for an optional two ounce trigger. The barrel is unblued stainless steel, with the option of ¾ or ⅞ inch barrel diameter. The larger barrel adds approximately two additional pounds of weight, which I prefer for better stability on the sand bags. The 40-XB comes with target scope blocks, but the receiver is also drilled and tapped for standard scope mounting.

I chose Jim Peightal (#6 8th St., Ernest, PA 15739—Phone 412-349-5216) to perform the job of marrying my 40-XB barreled action with the Lee Six weighted fiberglass Shilen Classic. I was impressed with three pieces of fiberglass stock work Peightal had turned out, a thumb-hole 22-250 (Ruger 77) he'd done for Helen Lewis (painted white), a thumbhole 228 Ackley Jim had done for Don Lewis (painted blaze orange) and a 7mm-08 Jim had done as an example to show what he could do in making up a classic, ultra-light big game rifle. This latter one was pigmented brown.

While working with fiberglass appears to be easier than working with walnut, fiberglass is no snap; plus it presents its own set of problems. The ease of working with fiberglass is how it sands. Excess material can be removed quickly and accurately, especially with electrically operated tools. However air pockets occasionally occur in the fiberglass. When these are sanded, large pits result. This is a particular problem if the fiberglass is going to be painted. The exterior surface must be almost as smooth as walnut prior to application of the stock finish. Any time air pockets are encountered during this final sanding and working of fiberglass, it means a filling procedure to allow the filler to dry—more laborious sanding.

Before any exterior stock work begins, the barreled action must be precisely fitted. Here Peightal used common liquid glass bedding compound after gouging out enough material that the 40-XB fit snuggly into my Shilen Classic.

For sand bag shooting one of the most important aids is a flat fore-end. While my Shilen Classic came with a flat fore-end, Jim Peightal made it even wider and flatter. Mine is just shy of three inches wide where it sits on the bag. This is an important consideration for those interested in true extra long range work with chucks.

Peightal also worked the trigger over patiently. It now goes off at a consistent 1½ pounds. Neither of us could wait to shoot it. Before the exterior was final sanded for painting, we met for a session off a makeshift bench. Though I didn't have a tape, I guessed the spread at ⅞ of an inch—a five shotter. Jim decided it might shoot better if he glass bedded the barrel the full length of the stock. This he did, finished the final sanding, added a soft Pachmayr Deluxe pad and sent it off to the painter for its blaze orange dousing. Glossy and even, I love this unusual paint job and shade.

I had a Weaver K12 with their discontinued Rangefinder reticle (the one with two horizontal crosswires six minutes apart). It was installed on Weaver bases and rings. The rig, as described, swung my baby scale needle around to fifteen pounds fifteen ounces. I brought the rig home one day from Peightal's, sighted it in, and headed for an all day chuck hunt the next morning with buddy Rich Drury.

Rich, an ardent upland hunter and outstanding shotgunner, had never previously shot woodchucks. That day we fired the new 25-06 40-XB a total of 53 times, almost exclusively at extra long range chucks. Rich made two very long shots for a tyro, one of which I was able to pace off—432 long steps. I wonder if that might be a record distance shot by someone who was chucking for their very first time? It proved to me that my choice of long range rifle ordnance was an excellent one.

I christened the 40-XB's existence with a rather easy shot, 250 at the outside. The 100 grain Sierra literally tore the chuck from its perch at the hole's entrance. There wasn't much to gloat over with that one, but the next time it was my turn I leveled on a pig much farther up the valley slope. If he wasn't five hundred yards, he was within a whisker of that distance. I bowled that one over with the first try. That chuck was something to gloat over, at least inwardly.

Later in the day we did a lot of shooting beyond five hundred yards, putting this 25-06 to the test with a great many pigs that were out and foraging that afternoon. At the extreme distance we did miss our share, but we were consistently close if we didn't score. Very seldom would we get a second try immediately. Our first shots were whizzing in such close proximity that the chucks were diving instantly for their burrows. On many occasions they'd come back out after only a brief stay subsurface. One more shot though, and we sent them scurrying back for subterranean safety.

The day prior to writing this chapter Don Lewis and I enjoyed a chuck hunt together, but weather conditions were miserable. It poured rain the whole way to our destination; then didn't stop too often all day long. We had to glass with binoculars through either rain, mist or both, then lie down in soaked grass when it came time to shoot. In such weather chucks can't be expected to be out and foraging much. We did manage to shoot at seven or eight that rainy day, and we bagged a quintet—Don three, me two. Lewis has been gunning chucks for more years than he cares to admit, and he's not all that impressed with this pig rig or that one. Though he wasn't gushy with his comments about my 40-X (that weighed so much), I know he was impressed. The first pig he tried took the 100 grain Sierra pill square in the neck— at beyond three hundred yards. Late in the day he tried one of those tough shots with only the chuck's head appearing above the recently excavated hole. The critter was simply enjoying the evening air or patiently checking out the surroundings before emerging further topside for a bellyful of tender alfalfa shoots. The range was again well beyond three hundred, with very little of the chuck showing, but Lewis managed to somersault him back out of the hole with a perfectly placed shot.

It was one of those days when the hay was high and it was extra tough for the observer to call the shots when the gunner missed. I was trying a pig at close to five hundred, with very little brown showing above the twelve inch high hay, but it was almost useless to shoot. The bullet would hit the grass, giving little indication whether the bullet was a bit high, a bit low, a bit left or a bit right. Some day I hope to get the experienced Don Lewis out when we'll be able to try a large number of shots in the five hundred yard range when calling the shots will be easier. I know then he'll be even more impressed with this specialized 40-XB.

I'm not trying to convey that this Remington 40-XB with Six fiberglass stock is the ultimate. Though what I've come up with is food for thought for readers, this chapter is also designed to both encourage you to conjure up your own version of a specialized varmint rifle that ideally suits your purposes. Frankly, I'm already thinking about yet another extra long range rig. It may be even heavier than this fifteen pound fifteen ouncer. I'm considering four cartridge choices, the standard 270 Win., the 6.5mm-06, the 7mm Rem. Mag. and the 30-338.

Whichever of the four I decide upon for my next varminter, you can bet the barrel will be a bull job—at least ⅞ inch in diameter. Though I might be dissuaded from fiberglass for the next one, it's doubtful. While I love the bright blaze orange stock of the current 40-XB 25-06, it's unique enough that I think I'd opt for something different with my next one—perhaps a pigmented fiberglass stock, but I'm just obtrusive and scatterbrained enough to consider bright blue or red!

If it turns out to be the 6.5-06 I'll probably opt for a 270 necked down case rather than a necked down 30-06 case, thus the gun will have to be chambered accordingly. The stronger 270 case will make maximum loads safer, and I feel max velocity loads are essential due to the extreme advantage of flatter trajectory.

With the 6.5-270 I'd try the 120 grain Sierra Spitzer first. The 140 grain Sierra Spitzer Boat Tail would be my second choice, but it's almost a lead pipe cinch that the long range trajectory of the 120 grain would be considerably flatter.

Of course the 6.5-270 would be very close to the 264 Winchester Magnum ballistically. It might be easier to have a barreled action chambered for this cartridge. In the long run I wonder if brass availability in 270 won't be plentiful for many years—compared to the less popular 264. No doubt 264 brass could be formed from 300 Win. Mag. brass, for the same case is used for both.

Many gunsmiths would have reamers for the 270, and I firmly believe it would be an excellent choice for extra long range chuck shooting. I have a good supply of 130 grain Remington Bronze Points in 270. I know this bullet style to be very accurate, that it maintains velocity as good or better than any other bullet on the market, and that it expands with super rapidity, even at the extreme distances. Unfortunately Remington no longer sells bullets to reloaders. My second choice would be the Sierra 130 grain Spitzer Boat Tail. This one's down range ballistics will be excellent. Whether or not it will open quickly enough on chucks at long range is a question mark, though I believe it will.

The 7mm Rem. Mag. is another cartridge for which the average gunsmith will have reamers on hand. So far it hasn't been picked up by varmint hunters as a possible one for extra long range work. Though I'm not an exponent of hollow point bullets for super distance work, I'd be willing to give the Sierra 168 grain Matchking Hollow Point a long try if using the 7mm Mag. in a heavy barreled extra long range rifle. A possible problem would be how heavy such a rifle would have to be so as to make recoil unobjectionable.

The same can be said from a recoil standpoint of the 30-338—how heavy would such a rig have to be and still be capable of true precision work at extra long range? Here I think I'd consider the Six fiberglass Benchrest Unlimited stock and go for something like two to four added pounds of weight. This would probably result in a rifle weighing close to twenty pounds. There are lots of 30 caliber bullets of bench rest quality available. The 30-338 offers outstanding possibilities for the extra long range minded.

Even though I consider my custom 40-XB 25-06 superb for the distance chuck shooting that is so dear to my heart, I'm not going to quit experimenting. Guess I'll always be messing around with yet another chuck rifle, for it's this experimentation that keeps up our constant interest in improvement and precision.

CHAPTER 4

Varmint Rifle Scopes

Even though the 250/3000 was introduced way back in 1915, it wasn't thought of much as a varmint cartridge. At that time the average hunter didn't have access to a telescopic sight. Varmint hunting, what little of it was practiced way back then, was an iron sight deal, and potting something as small as a woodchuck at anything much beyond a hundred yards with open sights was just as difficult then as it is today.

Even when the 22/250 Varminter came on the scene in the 1920's, only a few scopes were available. These then novel sights graced only the occasional gun shop shelf. Early scope imports, mostly from Germany, were of low power for long range varmint hunting requirements, and mounting them was a hassle. Drilled and tapped receivers, scores of different bases to match almost any receiver, and rings to mount the scopes in had hardly been thought of.

A smattering of scope sights were used as early as the Civil War. Yet their use was not only minimal, the average early day sportsman never even knew they were around, let alone had access to one. The result of all the foregoing was that varmint hunting was almost never practiced. Most of our country's citizens then worked six or more days a week, plus long ten and twelve hour days, just to keep bread on the table and bill collectors from foreclosing. Time for recreation was unheard of for many.

Varmint hunting started to roll in the 1930's, though only a handful of shooters were involved. A number of varmint cartridges were introduced, mainly on falling block type actions. Sporting scopes began making their way into a few of the sophisticated gun shops. World War II, during the first half of the 1940's, brought world chaos with it. During this period varmint hunting and improved scopes to go with them hardly crossed the average outdoorsman's mind.

Then came the 1950's with free time, added income, the Remington 222 cartridge, and inexpensive scopes from Bill Weaver of El Paso, Texas. Varmint hunting as we know it today was out of the starting gate. Today the American varmint hunter has an almost endless array of telescopic sights from which to choose—different models, different types, different powers.

From the 1950's onward, chuck hunters in the know outfitted their best varmint rifles with "target type" telescopic sights. These consisted of long tubes, large objective lenses (some as large as two inches in diameter), external adjustments, recoil springs, and they were mounted on target blocks—one block on the receiver—the other far out on the barrel. These were the very best one could use for distance work. Some still claim these target scopes are the best. Those who do swear by those made by the John Unertl Company, a small firm the average outdoorsman has never heard of, but a name synonymous with quality in the eyes of knowing varmint hunters.

Today there's a shift from long tubed varmint scopes mounted on target blocks to high powered scopes mounted on the receiver. We can thank the bench rest and silhouette crowds for this move. They demanded receiver mounted scopes that were lighter (to meet their various gun class specifications), but scopes that were equal or better than the longer and heavier target type glass. Even before this trend started there were several excellent receiver mounted scopes specifically for varmint hunting, but the shooting gentry has only recently realized how good they are. While target type scopes still have their champions, and perhaps always will, receiver mounted types are the varmint scopes of the future.

Only a few decades back the varmint hunter's problem was locating just one scope so he'd have something to attach to his new varmint rifle, today's problem is that of which to choose. The first choice facing the prospective buyer is one of power—which one is best suited for him, or should he select a variable power scope? We should assume that the choice of cartridge and rifle has already been made (before the scope).

Power choice should be in line with the maximum distance you intend shooting woodchucks. The trajectory of your cartridge is the controlling factor here. If too much scope power is selected, vibrations while sighting will be magnified. Also, mirage caused by heat waves could distort the sight picture so badly with high powered scopes that precision shooting becomes next to impossible. In short range situations a 6X can be okay for smallish targets, but I tend to lean toward

8X as my minimal power for varmints. I've used both 16X and 20X for extra long range work, but I find them too much, especially from a heat wave point of view. When trying to shoot into a hillside with the sun behind it, a sunshade on a scope is essential. The higher powers tend to magnify this problem. Some bench rest shooters swear by the higher powers, but they're trying to produce one hole groups in a highly controlled situation, compared to varmint hunters trying to secure the proper picture in all manner of varying light and background conditions.

While the 8X is suitable for two hundred, even 250 yard shooting, the 10X is better, unless heat waves are particularly bad. In this situation a drop back to eight power could improve one's shooting. For distance chuck work, what many varmint hunters are consummately interested in, the 12X is near perfect, though there are some who would claim the 15X can be even better under certain conditions.

Bill Weaver got telescopic sights off the ground in this country, starting his company back in 1933. That was the year he came out with his Model 330. I've always been partial to Weaver scopes. His line is varied, offering most anything either a varmint hunter or a big game hunter would want. Let's continue this chapter with a rundown of the possible varmint hunting scope considerations available as of this writing—starting with the Weavers.

WEAVER

The Weaver scope I liked best for varmint hunting, the 12X with Range Finder Reticle, was discontinued in 1981. It was their K Model. The only K Model they currently produce that's relatively ideal for varmints is their K856. This one's an eight power with a huge objective lens (56mm), almost 2½ inches. It has great light gathering power during low light level conditions and is wonderfully clear. It has ¼ minute click adjustments. Mine has Weaver's Dual X reticle, but the K856 can also be had in standard crosshair, post and crosshair, dot and German Post.

Weaver's T Models came about because silhouette shooters demanded receiver mounted scopes with external adjustments, so their sights could be readjusted quickly and accurately when changing shooting yardages at matches. Varmint hunters like these silhouette scopes, though I'm always leary that one of my prankster hunting buddies will spin those exposed scope knobs when I'm not looking. I have one of Weaver's T Models in 16X that I've used for a couple of years. New for 1982 was the Model KT10, this one with covered knobs. Mine is in Fine Crosshair. It also comes in Dual X, Standard Crosshair and Dot. Earlier Weaver introduced the KT6 and KT16, these two with

Weaver KT10

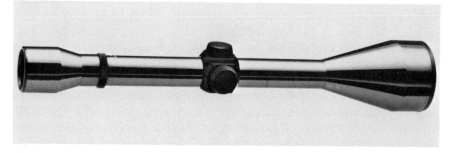

Weaver K856

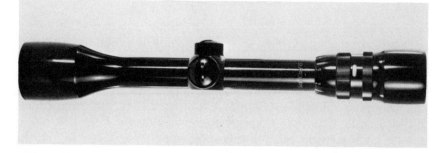

Bushnell 3X–9X ScopeChief *Wide Angle with PRF and BDC Model 70-390S.*

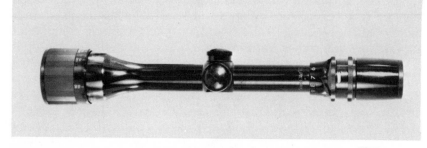

Bushnell 4X–12X (40mm) ScopeChief *with PRF and BDC. Model 70-M129.*

turret caps covering the scope adjustment knobs. Keep in mind that a prankster hunting buddy is not the only way to move exposed adjustment knobs. This can happen inadvertently, as when removing or returning the scope from or to its case or the vehicle. T Models come in 6X, 10X, 16X and 25X.

Don't sell any scope manufacturer's 3X-9X scopes short for varmint hunting, especially for varmint hunting out to two hundred yards, perhaps a little beyond. Weaver offers three different 3X-9X scopes, their Wider-View, their standard V Model, and their Auto-Comp. The latter is their bullet trajectory compensation type, variations of which are offered by a number of manufacturers.

BUSHNELL

Another of my favorite scope lines is the Bushnell. Like Weaver, they make several different models and powers for varmint hunting consideration. Picking up where we left off with Weaver, don't write the Bushnell 3X-9X scopes off as varmint getters. The top of the line is their ScopeChief 3X-9X. An option is their Prismatic Rangefinder and Bullet Drop Compensator. The Bushnell Banner line has three choices in the 3X-9X Variables, one with a 40mm objective lens, a wide angle with a 38mm objective lens, plus one with a 32mm objective lens. All Bushnell scopes feature their Multi-X reticle, even those with the Prismatic Rangefinder.

I have their Bushnell Banner 4X-12X Variable on my heavy barrel Savage 112V in 220 Swift. This one has the Prismatic Rangefinder and Bullet Drop Compensator feature. This type variable will also make a good choice for some combination varmint/big game outfits. It weighs only 1.5 to 2.5 ounces more than the very popular 3X-9X variables available from many manufacturers. Parallax adjustment is included on the Banner 4X-12X objective lens end.

Of the Banner fixed powers consider their 10X. This may be the best scope in the Bushnell line for longer range varmint work. It does not come with the Prismatic Rangefinder feature, but it can be had with Bullet Drop Compensator and Wind Drift Compensator. It weighs fourteen ounces, has parallex adjustment, and is highly popular with silhouette shooters. With a 40mm objective lens it has plenty of light gathering power.

REDFIELD

This company has long been synonymous with high quality optics for big game and varmint rifles. For a decade or more they've been bending over backwards with top scope choices for the varmint hunter, perhaps prompted by bench rest and silhouette shooters.

Redfield ILLUMINATOR

Redfield ILLUMINATOR
3X-9X Traditional

Redfield ILLUMINATOR
3X-9X Widefield

The top of the Redfield varmint scope line is their 6400 series. This one has exposed knobs, but like the Weaver T Models, mounts on the receiver rather than target blocks. The buyer has the option of either ⅛ or ¼ minute click adjustments, and the option of 16X, 20X or 24X. All 6400's come with Fine Crosshair. This one only weighs eighteen ounces.

Redfield's MS/Varmint models come in 8X, 10X and 12X, but only their 4 Plex reticle is available. These type reticles are almost impossible to use for extremely long range shooting situations, five hundred yards and longer. This is because bullet trajectory falls off so far at these extreme distances that the woodchuck can be covered by the thicker portion of this type reticle. Of course tapered crosshair type reticles with a bullet drop type compensator can be adjusted to the proper range before firing—with the shooter holding the crosshairs right on the target. Wind compensations must still be made.

Redfield's answer to range estimation is called *Accu-Trac*. By zooming the power ring of a variable scope to match a standing chuck (approximately eighteen inches) the range is then read on a scale in the bottom of the scope. The elevation knob is then quickly spun to that distance, the shooter holds the crosswires right on the chuck. Just before the shot one can even increase to full power before squeezing the trigger.

Two top varmint choices with *Accu-Trac* are the Traditional Variables—the 4X-12X and the 6X-18X. These weigh fourteen and eighteen ounces respectively, have plenty of eye relief and a two-inch objective lens for plenty of light gathering. I have a 6X-18X with *Accu-Trac* mounted on my 112V Savage in 25-06. It's amazing how compact this scope is and still capable of eighteen power. The 6400 is longer, but no heavier.

In their 3X-9X Variables Redfield offers three different lines, then different types within those lines. Their top model is the Illuminator. Through an ingenious lens system the user can see the target area with more brilliance. It comes in either Traditional or Widefield style, and *Accu-Trac* is available on both.

Next is the Redfield Traditional Model in 3X-9X. In addition to the standard style, there's also the Royal, this one with ½ inch additional eye relief—excellent for hard recoiling calibers. Both these Traditional 3X-9X scopes are available with or without *Accu-Trac*. The Low Profile Redfield 3X-9X also comes with or without *Accu-Trac*. Finally, there's the Tracker Model, Redfield's inexpensive line. It comes in 3X-9X, but there's no *Accu-Trac* option.

Since a great deal of space is being given to the 3X-9X scope as a possibility for varmint hunting, including the previous two paragraphs about the Redfields, this is a good time to expound on the suggestion. The 3X-9X is not the scope for a heavy barreled 6mm, 25-06, 6.5-06 or 270. This variable is at its best on a lighter rifle that the owner will want to use as a combination gun for big game and woodchucks. Some suggested possibilities for this would be a standard weight 243 Win., a 6mm Rem., 257 Roberts, a 250/3000, etc. Couple these cartridges with the 3X-9X scope and light rifles like the Remington 700 BDL or ADL, the Ruger 77, the Winchester Model 70, the Smith & Wesson Model 1500, the Interarms Mark X, the Sako Sporter, the Savage 110, the Weatherby Vanguard, the Browning Lightning Bolt and similar rigs that'll weigh around eight pounds scoped, and you have an excellent combo.

LEUPOLD

This Oregon based company produces extremely high quality scopes, and they have some interesting possibilities for woodchuck enthusiasts. They're one of the few who offer the option of an adjustable objective lens (for parallex) in a 3X-9X scope. They call this one the Vari-X II. It's also available without the parallex adjustment, but serious chuck hunters will opt for the parallex adjustment feature. Another innovative model from Leupold is their Vari-X III in 3.5X-10X. It, too, is available with and without the adjustable objective lens. A most interesting possibility is their Vari-X III 6.5X-20X which comes only with the adjustable objective lens.

Leupold's M8 series is ideally suited to varmint use, at least those of 8X and above. They come in 8X, 12X, 24X and 36X. All Leupold scopes, with the exception of the M8 36X come with three choices of reticles—the Duplex, the Dot, and the CPC. This latter one features two slowly tapering crosswires.

73

LYMAN

Lyman, the Connecticut based firm that makes a number of outdoor products, is the manufacturer of several excellent telescopic sights. Their bench resters come in 20X, 25X and 35X. With these there are four choices of reticles, Standard Fine Crosswire, Extra Fine Crosswire, ¼ Minute Dot, and ⅛ Minute Dot. This company also offers 8X and 10X scopes for woodchucksters, with and without covered scope adjustment knobs. I must prefer the covered type for varmint shooting. Finally, there's the Lyman 3X-9X Variable. It and the 8X and 10X Lymans come with either Standard Crosswire, Center Range (Duplex), 1 Minute Dot or ½ Minute Dot.

BURRIS

In 1977 Burris introduced their *Hi-Lume* scope lenses. They claim them to be the brightest and most glare free in the business. I had a 3X-9X Burris Variable which was excellent. In addition to the regular 3X-9X variable, Burris also offers 4X-12X and 6X-18X Variables for varmint hunting consideration. These are offered in Plex, fine crosshair and .7-2 inch dot. I considered the latter too large for distant work on anything but big game animals.

Burris also offers fixed power varmint scope sights, a 10X and a 12X. Choice is Plex, fine crosshair or ½ Minute Dot. Both have objective end parallex adjustments, as do their 4X-12X and 6X-18X Variables. The 3X-9X Variable does not have a parallex adjustment. Scopes without external parallex adjustment are set to be parallex free at some medium range.

Burris offers two choices of compensating reticles in two special 3X-9X models. I consider them both better suited to big game work because of the size of the dot. Other companies' bullet drop compensators work similarly. The rig is sighted in for two hundred yards. The calibrated range ring is then installed. The company supplies three

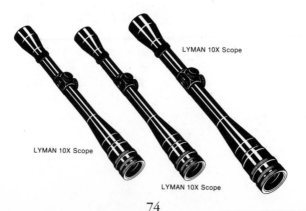

LYMAN 10X Scope

LYMAN 10X Scope

LYMAN 10X Scope

different rings. You install the one that matches the trajectory of the cartridge and bullet you're using. Estimate the yardage by dialing it on the calibrated ring. The crosshair moves up (apparently) remaining zeroed for two hundred yards, but the dot moves down, assuming you've estimated a significantly longer range, say four hundred yards. You then hold the dot on the target area and pull the trigger. As mentioned previously, the dot is likely to block out the woodchuck completely at four hundred yards and beyond. Of course 3X-9X scopes weren't and aren't intended for this distance work. They dub this scope the 3X-9X ARC.

The second Burris range finder scope is called the 3X-9X RAC. It incorporates the feature described in the paragraph preceding, plus two stradia width crosswires at the bottom of the scope's field. You match the standing chuck between these two wires by moving the vari-power ring to more or less power. The dot is set for the proper yardage after the power ring and matching of stradia lines have helped you determine the distance. This one is also better suited to big game.

SWIFT

This import company of good Japanese made scopes does not cater to the varmint hunter. Their highest powered fixed power scope is a 6X. They do have two 3X-9X's, one with a 32mm objective lens, the other a 40mm wide angle. In it one can opt for standard crosshair or Quadraplex, plus the Bullet Drop Compensator.

JASON/EMPIRE

This is another Japanese scope importer, and their 3X-9X's are the only ones for varmint hunters to consider, and then only on rifles that can be used for both big game and chucks. They have 3X-9X's with 32mm wide angle, 32mm standard and 40mm for extra light gathering.

SWAROVSKI

This one is made in Austria, and it's a dandy. Unfortunately 6X is the highest power currently available. Four different reticles are offered, but the Swarovski is a bit shy in power for use in most woodchuck hunting.

L. M. DICKSON

This is another import company. They offer two 3X-9X possibilities, one with a 32mm objective lens, the other with a 40mm.

DAVIS OPTICAL

This company offers relatively inexpensive target scopes for attaching to target blocks on receiver and barrel. I have never examined a Davis. They were formerly R. A. Litschert.

Their target model scopes come with either 1¼ or 1½ inch objective lenses, fully adjustable for parallax. The 1¼ inch Davis is called the Spot Shot. It's available in 10X, 12X, 15X and 20X. The 1½ inch Davis is called the New Spot Shot. It comes in 10X, 12X, 15X, 20X, 25X and 30X. Options include a ten inch lens shade, extra fine crosshairs and recoil spring. They weigh nineteen and twenty ounces respectively.

TASCO

This is another Japanese importer based in Miami. Tasco offers both range finding trajectory and trajectory compensating scopes. There are a number of 3X-9X models, plus one variable of higher power, a 6X-18X. Note that most all variables zoom up to about three times minimal power.

WHAT TYPE OF RETICLE IS BEST?

As mentioned in the Weaver scope section, I like the two horizontal crosswires—their discontinued Range Finder Reticle. For extra long range chuck shooting the bottom crosswire gives a better reference point for holding on subsequent shots, especially after your hunting partner calls where your bullet struck after the first shot (or ensuing ones). You remember where you held with more precision if you use two horizontal wires, then you can compensate with more precision and bring the second shot closer, if not make a telling one.

No one currently offers two horizontal crosswires. The bottom wire in the Weaver Range Finder is six minutes of an angle below the upper wire, the one you use to zero. That means 24 inch difference at 400 yards, 30 inches at 500, 36 inches at 600. At these distant ranges that bottom crosswire can be of extreme benefit. However, crosswires that are four minutes of an angle apart could be even better, for they'd be only 16 inches apart at 400 yards, 20 inches at 500, 24 inches at 600. At 400 and 500 yards an extremely flat shooting rifle will permit the shooter to hold closer to the chuck with the bottom wire. This more precise aiming reference, the bottom wire, is what makes a two horizontal wire scope so ideal for those extra long range shots.

For true distance work, lacking the Weaver Range Finder type reticle, what would be my choice? It could be that one of the new fangled range estimating and/or bullet drop compensating scopes will be the ticket, but I don't have enough experience with them yet. I'm still trying to form an opinion. My initial thought is that they're more suited to big game than small varmints like woodchucks. Whether we chuck specialists will be able to adjust to them still remains a question.

Dot reticles are generally too big, but extremely small ones should be considered and are available from a few manufacturers. I haven't tried these super small ones yet—some day! The "duplex" type reticle is fine for up to about two hundred yards, maybe a little more, depending upon cartridge trajectory. For extreme ranges the thick portion of the lower vertical wire covers all or too much of the little chuck target. I do like this reticle on rifles intended for the shorter ranges, and on light combo big game/varmint rigs.

Finally, the very thin crosswire varminters have been using for years is still an excellent one. No one will go wrong making this reticle choice for long range work, assuming the scope he wants is offered with extra fine crosshair. Some of them are not.

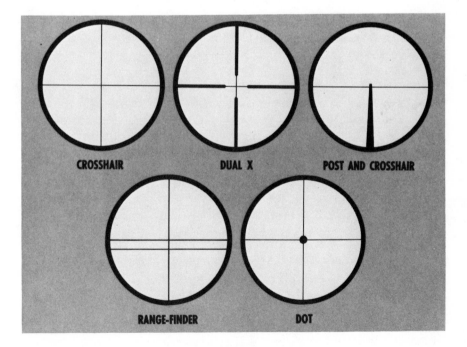

CROSSHAIR   DUAL X   POST AND CROSSHAIR

RANGE-FINDER   DOT

Weaver Reticles

Sisley levels on a chuck with a favorite varmint rifle, the Savage 112V in 220 Swift.

CHAPTER 5

Cartridges, Calibers and Proper Bullets

This chapter is devoted to cartridges and loads that are ideal, or almost ideal, for general varmint hunting, mainly for woodchucks, but also for prairie dogs and crows. This list of cartridges is a long one. More information will be provided for those used most commonly, less information for cartridges that will see minimal use on varmints.

Today's sportsman is blessed with choice after choice of cartridges in what many consider the ideal varmint caliber—the 22 centerfire. Most bullets in this category are .224 in diameter.

THE 22 HORNET

Though few rifles besides the Ruger #3 single shot are currently available in 22 Hornet, old Hornets still on gun racks keep shooting; thus the demand for factory loads and bullets for reloading. The Hornet (the first centerfire for varmint shooting) can still hold its own at reasonably short ranges. Its predecessor was the 22 WCF, a black powder 22 centerfire. The Hornet was a "wildcat." Winchester began offering Hornet factory ammo in 1930. By 1932 Savage had the first factory rifle for it—the Model 23 D. A year later Winchester offered the Hornet in their Model 54 bolt action. Factory velocities are close to 2700 fps with a 45 grain bullet. This lighter pill is suggested for reloaders. The 50 to 55 grain .224 bullets are better suited to centerfires with more velocity than the Hornet. Maximum Hornet velocity for the 55 grain bullet is down to about 2300 fps.

The Hornet's forte is mild report and fine accuracy. Though not a long range cartridge, it does very well out to 150, maybe 175 yards. Some of the old Hornets wore barrels only safely suited to .223 bullets. Sierra offers 40 and 45 grain bullets—in both .223 and .224—the former for shooters who need that slightly smaller pill.

Since the Hornet has limited case capacity, relatively fast burning powders are best suited. Try Hodgdon 110, Winchester 296, Hercules 2400 or 1MR227. The 22 Hornet case is a rimmed one, thus it's ideal for the Ruger #3 falling block type action. Case length should be a mere 1.338 inches.

THE 22 K HORNET

The 22 K Hornet was the brainchild of Lysle Kilbourn, a northern New York State gunsmith who fire-formed regular Hornet cases in a chamber he had opened up. The Hornet, with soft brass, opened beautifully, so Kilbourn came up with a case which had more powder capacity. He was successful in stepping up 45 grain bullet velocity to over 3,000 fps. Interestingly, the 22 K Hornet was one of the first cartridges to be "improved" (fire forming to increase case capacity). After the Hornet was improved, cartridge after cartridge was developed using the same basic idea. Earlier the Hornet had also been a trend setter, having been developed by "custom tinkerers." Factory ammo was offered later, then factory rifles.

218 BEE

The Bee upstaged the Hornet, arriving on the shooting scene in 1938. It is based on necking down the 32/20 black powder cartridge. Being a rimmed case, it was favored by some who thought highly of single shot, falling block type actions. But keep in mind their popularity was never all that much. Today the Bee is about dead, hardly quivering. None the less, it was and is an effective varmint gun out to 150 yards. Winchester still makes factory ammo for the 218 Bee, a 46 grain OPE that departs the muzzle at 2,760 fps.

219 ZIPPER

The Zipper came out a year prior to the Bee. Also on a rimmed case, it never enjoyed a great deal of popularity, though velocities were up considerably over the Bee and Hornet. Forty-five grain bullets could be driven up to 3,600 fps if used in certain custom bolt action rifles.

Such hot loads were not recommended in the lever guns—like the 336 Marlin, which was produced in the 219 Zipper until 1961. A good powder choice is 4320, and heavier bullets like the 55 grainers are fine.

219 DONALDSON WASP

After five or more years of tinkering, Harvey Donaldson announced this namesake. It was extremely popular until the 1950's, when the 222 Remington arrived on the shooting scene and stole its thunder. The rimmed cases are made by shortening and blowing out 219 Zipper cases, a somewhat tedious task, but in the 40's the Wasp was a consistent bench rest winner, plus took its toll on thousands of wary woodchucks. It's pretty much a dead injun today. There was also a rimless version of the Wasp.

222 REMINGTON

If one modern day cartridge has taken varmint hunting by storm and made varmint hunting what it is today, a great many knowledgeable chuck hunters would vote for this one. The "deuce" was born in 1950, when it was chambered for the company's Model 722 bolt gun. With quick dispatch the rest of the gun makers jumped on the 222 band wagon. It's not a necked down or blown out anything, but a cartridge of original design. If the wind isn't blowing too much, the 222 is absolutely lethal on chucks at 200 and 250 yards. If the accurate bolt gun is topped with a high quality scope of say 8X or 10X, the quarry doesn't have much of a chance. The 222 Remington is that good.

The cartridge is at its best with 50 to 55 grain bullets carefully squeezed into its neck. Bench rest shooters compiled some amazing records with this fine little cartridge, though by and large they've come to choose other cartridges today. While earlier experimenters in the 22 centerfire realm had consistently chosen rimmed cases to fool with, Remington decided to come up with a rimless 22 centerfire cartridge—so the 222 Remington was the first of these.

One of the best powders for reloaders to consider is 4198, though BL-C is also an excellent consideration. Top velocity with 50 grain bullets is in the 3,200 fps realm, about the same for the 52 grainers, a hundred foot seconds less for 55 grain fodder.

222 REMINGTON MAGNUM

Its Magnum stepson was introduced eight years later—a result of Remington's experiments for the military. The main difference in the two is the Magnum case is .015 inches longer, resulting in more powder capacity. The 50 grain bullets can be driven 100 to 200 fps faster. Ditto for the 52, 53 and 55 grain bullets. Even the 63 grain Sierra can be stepped up to over 3,000 fps if 4198 is used. Slightly slower burning powders are usually better in the 222 Magnum, though, such as 4895, 4064 and 3031. Very few gun manufacturers offer the 222 Mag. today, but many offer the regular "deuce." Chances are good the 222 will retain its popularity, but if it doesn't, the following cartridge will be responsible for its demise, as that cartridge has sung the funeral death dirge for the 222 Remington Magnum.

223 REMINGTON

Remington was working with at least two cartridges aimed at the military in the late 50's. Both were to fire light .224 inch bullets in semi-automatic weapons. The army brass had determined that the average soldier couldn't handle the recoil the M-1 and 30/06 put out, especially when a great deal of fire power was required to "keep the enemy down!" They wanted a 22 centerfire that belched tiny 50 or 55 grain pills with near machine gun regularity. The 222 Remington Magnum and 223 Remington were those two experimental cartridges. The 223 Remington finally won out. Around 1957 or 1958 it became known around the world as the 5.56mm. Our military uses this cartridge today in the AR-15.

It would be splitting hairs to say that the 222 Remington might have a slight accuracy edge over the 223, or that the miniscule larger case capacity of the 222 Rem. Magnum means bullets can be driven at higher velocity. The bottom line is that for varmint hunting, the 223 is plenty fast and accurate enough in a good bolt rifle. You'll find it super inexpensive to shoot because surplus military brass is so cheap and readily available. Anyone scouring the pages of *SHOTGUN NEWS* will find many competitive ads—for cheap military fired brass.

Couple the facts that the brass for the 223 is cheap and readily available with the fact that numerous manufacturers offer excellent bolt guns in this chambering, and you can see why the 223 is so highly popular today. The 223 might be the most popular all around varmint caliber of the future.

Despite its name, the 223 is designed to fire bullets of .224 diameter. The best choices fall into the 50 to 55 grain realm. The 50 grainers can be safely driven to 3,300 and 3,400 fps with proper powders, the 52 and 53 grainers almost as fast, and the 55 grain pills can be spewed out at over 3,200 fps with certain powders.

Like its smaller cousin, the 222 Remington, the 223 digests 4198 very well. Winchester's Ball Powder 748 is also very good. BL-C and 3031 are also considerations.

Remington offers the 223 in the no-frills 788, the 700 BDL Varmint and their 40-XBBR. Sako offers it in both their Sporter and Heavy Barrel, Savage in its 340 clip repeater, Steyr-Mannlicher in its Model SL, Ruger in the Mini-14, and Ruger #3, Drico in its Model 6405 Match Sporter, and there are probably several others. The well rounded varmint hunter of the future will almost certainly have one or more 223 Remington guns on his wall rack.

225 WINCHESTER

This was the last "new" cartridge that Winchester introduced. Though company moguls might be quick to claim there is no reason for the introduction of new cartridges, Remington keeps introducing them—and successfully. Perhaps the fact that Winchester's 225 venture wasn't successful has soured the company from further cartridge development. The 225 came out in 1964 with at least some fanfare. Its tomb was sealed a year later when Remington announced the introduction of the 22/250 Varminter factory round. Finally 22/250 brass became readily available to any and all who wanted to try this wildcat, which had been extremely popular in custom guns for thirty years. The cheap availability of 223 brass and the popularity of that cartridge further sealed the 225's coffin. It is built on what the manufacturer calls a semi-rimless case. If you have a 225, you probably load 4064 powder, or you should. No manufacturer currently makes a rifle chambered for the 225 Winchester.

224 WEATHERBY MAGNUM

This cartridge is the only 22 centerfire that utilizes a belted case. Weatherby cases are expensive, so cost has deterred the 224 Weatherby from becoming more popular than it is. It was introduced in 1963, a year prior to the 225 Winchester, and is capable of ballistics that come close to the 22/250 Varminter. The case is quite strong. Try powders like 3031, Norma 201 and 4064.

22 PPC

This one was developed by the bench rest crowd, or rather two of their gender, Ferris Pindell and Dr. Lou Palmasano. This cartridge has never been offered for commercial rifles intended for varmint hunting. It is based on the 220 Russian case, and is noted for its outstanding accuracy. With the Hornady 53 grain Bench Rest Hollow Point, Norma 201's maximum load speeds the bullet along at 3,500 fps, so it's a fast stepper.

5.6 × 50 MAGNUM

This cartridge is slightly longer than the 222 Remington Magnum. No U.S. based companies make rifles for it or ever have. It can, however, shoot 50 grain bullets to 3,400 and 3,500 fps velocities, so it can't be bad mouthed. Try 4064 or Winchester 748.

5.6 × 57mm RWS

Like the cartridge above, this one was also born in Germany in the mid-60's. It is capable of even faster bullet speeds, but has never been popular for varmint hunting in America, nor will it be. Still, those who have a 5.6 × 57 have an excellent varmint getter.

22/250 VARMINTER (REMINGTON)

This is perhaps the greatest ground hog getter of all time, plus the Varminter has done plenty of damage to crow and prairie dog populations as well. The 22/250 is no spring chicken either. The 250 Savage was introduced way back in 1915, more popularly known as the 250/3000. Experimenters quickly began necking the case to accept .224 caliber bullets and chambering wildcat rifles for this new cartridge, but it was J. E. Gebby who copyrighted the name "Varminter."

Rifles of old had a number of different chamberings. With them caution must be used when reloading, staying well below suggested max loads. Current day 22-250's started in 1963 when Browning first chambered this wildcat cartridge in a factory rifle—even before commercially loaded ammo was available for it. Remington followed Browning's lead by offering factory ammo in 1965. They first chambered their 700 bolt gun for the 22/250 in 1967. Since then numerous other manufacturers have chambered all manner of rifles for this great cartridge.

Its potential for accuracy is excellent, especially for varmint hunters, but even bench resters have used the 22/250 effectively to win championships. This one sees its best potential with 50 to 55 grain bullets, and many have opted for the superbly accurate bench rest bullets in this weight realm. The Varminter is at its apex when loaded at about 3,700 fps with 50, 52 and 53 grain bullets, to around 3,600 fps with 55 grain bullets. Because of the high velocity, it's a flat shooter, which long range varminters are always most interested in seeing.

The optimal powder choices are 4064, 3031 and 4895. You should still experiment to find out which bullets and which powders any particular rifle handles best.

220 SWIFT

The gun writers of the 1930's didn't show the 220 Swift much respect. Many of them bad mouthed it to a considerable degree, so much that the Swift, said by some to be the ultimate 22 centerfire, died because of inaccurate pennings. Complaints in print varied from neck stretching to barrel throat erosion to accuracy problems to erratic pressures.

In the 1970's the Swift was resurrected, but I question how long its revitilized life will last. Savage offered it in their 112V, but has recently discontinued this heavy barreled bolt. Ruger still offers it in their Model 77 Heavy Barrel Varmint, but they're tough to find. Too bad that more varmint hunters will never shoot the Swift, nor see what it's capable of accomplishing. Everything the 22/250 can do the Swift can do better, but not much.

Throat erosion in the Swift can be largely reduced by cutting back velocity levels until they're similar to the 22/250. The case is a very strong one, based on the semi-rimmed 6mm Lee Navy. Winchester got velocity up to 4,000 fps by jamming lots of power in—until pressures were in the 55,000 psi range. The case could take it, but barrels didn't last long. Winchester began offering their Model 70 Swifts with a stainless steel barrel to quell the fears about barrel erosion, but the bad seed of early barrel wear had already been planted in too many rifleman's brains.

This is a long range cartridge par excellence, truly a 300 and 350 yard chuck gun, if the wind isn't blowing. Lots of chucks have been riddled by the Swift at even more distant ranges. There isn't a cartridge in the world that shoots flatter than a hot loaded Swift spewing a sharply pointed bullet.

SUMMARY OF 22 CALIBER CENTERFIRES

If I had to be restricted to only two 22 caliber centerfires for all my varmint hunting, I'd chose either the 222 Remington or the 223 Remington AND either the 22/250 or the 220 Swift. Narrowing the choice even further, cost of brass would probably cause me to chose the 223 over the 222. Future availability of the 22/250 cartridge and brass over the 220 Swift would probably prejudice my choice to the former.

There's no question that all four are superb varmint cartridges, but what if I had to choose only one 22 centerfire? What would it be? Me thinks the choice would have to be the 223 Remington. In some instances, especially during intensive prairie dog shooting, the 22/250 and the Swift create too much muzzle blast and too much recoil—and I'm talking about shooting boxes and boxes of shells in one day, not twenty or thirty rounds. Here the lower report and softer recoil of the 223 will begin to shine. To replace the 22/250 or Swift and for longer range work on various varmints, I'd opt for one of the 6mm's, a 25, even a 6.5mm.

17 REMINGTON

Calibers smaller than .224 will never be overly popular, even with varmint hunters; nevertheless, the 17 Remington is an excellent one—negligible recoil, soft report and inherent accuracy. The Remington and Hornady .172 diameter 25 grain hollow point bullets are extremely effective on chucks, prairie dogs and crows. I would not suggest they be used on larger animals.

The 17 Remington was introduced by the Ilion, New York, based firm in 1971—with both factory ammo and in their 700 BDL. I've toted mine on many a chuck hunt, and I've never been anything but favorably impressed with it. The 17 has also performed to perfection on prairie dogs. Factory ballistics speed the little 25 grain hollow point along at 4,000 fps, but my handloads of 22 grains of 4895 cut the speed back to about 3,750. The 17 is not a spectacular killer, like say a 25/06 at 200 yards with the 100 grain Sierra, but even at my reduced handload velocities, the 17 is plenty wicked enough.

The mild Remington 7½ primers must be used when loading this 17. It is based on the 223 Remington case, a version that is both necked down and shortened. It standardized some former 17/223 wildcats. The HORNADY HANDBOOK claims 4320 is the best powder for the 17.

There are several additional 17's—all wildcats, the 17/222 (obviously based on the 222 Rem. case), the 17 Mach IV (based on the 221 Rem.

The big 25-06 cartridge next to the rather diminutive 17mm Rem.

Fireball case), and the 17 Ackley Bee (based on the 218 case). The standardized 17 Remington offers the highest velocity potential of them all, and Remington still offers the 700 BDL in this cartridge.

5.6 × 52R (22 SAVAGE HIGH-POWER)

The 22 Savage High-power does not use the common .224 caliber bullets, but those of .227 diameter. Hornady is one manufacturer that offers a 70 grain Spire Point in .227. Charles Newton was the prime developer of this one, based on the 25/35 necked down. Maximum velocity with the 70 weight pill can be considerably over 3,000 fps, so it's a good one. Unfortunately no one offers a rifle in this caliber.

228 ACKLEY MAGNUM

This one also uses that special .227 70 grain Hornady Spire Point. Be certain never to use these larger diameter bullets with standard .224 centerfires. This high stepper is capable of pushing that 70 grain Hornady to over 3,400 fps.

The case is a necked down version of the 30/06, so brass is readily available. RCBS can make you up a set of dies. Though introduced way back in 1938, the .228 Ackley never gained much popularity, but there's a flicker of reinterest in this cartridge today, and well there should be, for it's a good one. My buddy, confirmed gun nut Don Lewis, has a 228, which Ackley did the metal work on. Then he had Six Enterprises provide a thumbhole fiberglass stock, which gunsmith Jim Peightal (pronounced PAY' tal) bedded. Don then had Jim paint the whole rig blaze orange, the perfect color for a chuck hunter's rifle.

243 WINCHESTER

When a breeze is blowing in chuck country and the critters to be shot at are 175 yards and beyond, the 6mm's are head and shoulders better than any 22 centerfire that ever coughed up a bullet. The reason is simply bullet weight—the 6's are heavier. Except in a stiff breeze, the 6's do extremely well out to 300, even 350 yards, compared to 50 and 55 grain .224 bullets. The 243 Winchester permitted the average chuck hunter to become a long range rifleman, not so much because of any improvement in trajectory, but through increased wind bucking powers.

The 243, introduced in 1955, is bound to stay around chuck hunting circles for a long, long time. Based on the .308 Win. case, brass is readily available, not only from the ammo manufacturers, but also from military surplus. It wasn't long after the 243 was introduced that virtually every rifle manufacturer had an offering or two. Well they should have. Warren Page, *Field and Stream's* Shooting Editor for many years, had a great deal to do with the popularity of the 6mm's. Not only did they serve up the long range chuck hunter exactly what he wanted and needed, these guns also doubled perfectly on deer and antelope. Some writers pooh-poohed the 6mm's worth on these larger game animals, but time has proven them wrong. The 243, and its Remington cousin, the 6mm Remington, are superb deer killers, and they have wonderfully mild recoil as deer guns go. You'll find that they recoil a bit more than the 22 centerfires.

For the chucksman the 243 is best with bullets of 80 to 85 grains. These can be safely driven in the 3,200 fps realm if the appropriate powders are selected. The 85 grain Sierra Spitzer and their 85 grain Hollow Point Boat Tail are two of the very best. Good powder choices are 4064 and 4350, though the 6's, with their increased case capacity, are not as powder finicky as some of the smallish .224 cartridges. Don't try reduced charges, especially if using the slower burning powders. Chuck hunters are seldom interested in reduced loads anyway. When it comes to a round for both chucks and bucks, there has never been a more popular one than the .243 Winchester.

6mm REMINGTON

The 244 Remington was introduced the same year as the 243 Winchester. Remington brass decided in some corporate meeting, wrongly, that the cartridge would be used only by chuck hunters shooting smallish bullets. Deer hunters loved the 6's and bought 'em. To their dismay the 244's 1-12 twist wouldn't stabilize the bullets the buck chasers liked—the 100 grainers. The 243, with its 1-10 twist, did stabilize the 100 grainers, plus the 80, 85 and 90 grain varmint bullets.

Remington finally went back to the drawing board to bring out a 244 with a 1-10 twist, renaming it the 6mm Remington. Evidently the damage had been done. The Remington round has never matched Winchester's in popularity. That's a pity, for the Remington is the better of the two. It can get another hundred foot seconds out of an eighty or 85 grain bullet, mostly because it has slightly larger case capacity.

The 6mm Rem. is interchangeable with the 244 Rem. No difference in the cartridge, only in the barrel twist. A tremendous number of factory rifles are available in both 243 and 6mm. You can consequently choose either. A browse through any catalog will quickly prove that practically any rifle model and any design can be purchased in 243 Win. or 6mm Rem., or both. Some of the least expensive and best suited chuck, crow and prairie dog guns are the heavy barrels currently offered by Ruger in their 77 Varmint (both 243 and 6mm offered), the Remington 700 BDL Varmint (both offered), Winchester Model 70 Varmint (243 offered) and the Ruger Number One Heavy Barrel Varmint (both offered).

Powders and bullets that work well in 243's work to perfection in the 6mm Rem. This is one of the best, easy accessible varmint cartridges available today.

240 WEATHERBY MAGNUM

This could be the best 6mm of the lot, but cases are too expensive and not as readily available. Roy Weatherby probably doesn't care since he no doubt makes money on his rifles rather than his ammo. While the 243 is based on the 308 Win. case, the 240 Wby. is based on the 30/06 case, a bigger one. The 240 sports a belt on the case, as all Weatherby Magnums do. It's capable of pushing 80 grain bullets to 3,700 fps with max charges of Win. 785, one of the best powders for the 240 Wby.

Weatherby cartridges have considerable space between the end of the normally seated bullet and the rifling, called freeboring. Varmint hunters can often improve accuracy in Weatherby rifles by seating hand loaded bullets to minimal depth, so the bullet tip is closer to the rifling when the action is closed. In some cases such longer-than-usual ammo won't depress into the magazine, but this is no problem for many varmint hunting situations—where one cartridge is loaded in the chamber only after one is actually preparing to shoot. No rounds are carried in the magazine anyway. Take care not to seat bullets out too far. If bullets engage the rifling after the bolt is closed and the shot is not taken, there's a good chance the bullet will pull out of the case, engaged in the rifling, and powder will spill everywhere upon case extraction. The gun will be out of commission until you can push the bullet out with a cleaning rod, plus you'll have a case full of powder to clean out of the action. Bullets seated minimally tend to raise chamber pressures, so cut back powder content on maximum loads.

6mm/284

The 284 Winchester is an excellent big game cartridge, but has never enjoyed its predicted popularity. Initially there were quite a number of fellows who necked down the 284 to 6 millimeters, my friend Bob Cassidy being one of them. I've watched Bob make some extra long range shots with this round. While it's a dandy, it'll never gain much more popularity. Any reader who has one already knows about this excellent cartridge's capabilities.

6 × 47

The bench rest fraternity came up with this one, but it's not seen often in summer chuck fields. Its accuracy potential is outstanding but falls short of the much more popular and readily available 243 and 6mm Rem. with regard to trajectory, always of primary importance to a long range varmint hunter. BL-C powder is suggested. The 6 × 47 is based on the 222 Remington case, simply necked up to 6mm.

6mm INTERNATIONAL

The 6mm International was developed by necking down the 250 Savage (250/3000) case. It comes very close to matching the 243 in velocity. Remington currently offers it in their 40-XB, and that rifle, though intended more for bench resters, is excellent in chuck country—no matter the caliber.

6mm PPC

Like the 22 PPC, this 6mm was developed by Dr. Lou Palmasano and Ferris Pindell. It's based on the same .220 Russian case as its little brother—necked up to 6mm. It pushes a 70 grain bullet in the 3,100 to 3,200 fps range. A championship performer with bench resters, you won't find many in chuck fields.

250/3000

Savage Arms would prefer everyone to call this one the 250 Savage, and some do, but the 250/3000 has a better ring to most of us, so that's the moniker most in use. The cartridge is best used as a combo varmint and whitetail outfit. Through the years it has mainly been available only in the lever Savage 99, and lever actions never have and never will make it with varmint hunters, even as a combination gun. Winchester offered the 250/3000 for a short time in both the Model 70 and Model 54, but it never caught fire. Today you're pretty much confined to custom gunsmiths if you want one in bolt rifles.

Based on the 30/06 case, this necked down version is shortened appreciably, so much so that it can be used in so-called "short action" bolt guns. Charlie Newton was the designer. The "3000" in the name comes from the fact that it was supposed to be the first cartridge with 100 grain bullets that'd get 3,000 fps. In reality they had to use an 87 grainer to hit the three thou mark on the chronograph. With the introduction of Winchester's 243, the 250/3000 sort of sputtered its last, though good rifles still make occasional sojourns to summer chuck fields and dog town edges.

257 ROBERTS

Here's an excellent varmint cartridge, and another that doubles well on deer hunts, though its maximum range should be kept to around two hundred yards for big game work. Thankfully the 257 Roberts appears to be making a comeback. First Ruger offered a limited run of them in 1972 with their Model 77. In 1981 Winchester announced it would be one of six offerings in their bring back of the Model 70 Featherweight. In 1982 Remington announced a limited run of 257's for their Model 700 Classic—and the "short action" version to boot.

Ned Roberts developed this one, but Remington standardized it in 1934, at the same time offering it in their Model 30-S bolt rifle. It's at its varmint best with 87 to 100 grain bullets—the latter can be pushed to 3,000 fps, but only with max loads using certain powders. Hornady's max load of 4895 pushes that company's 87 grain Spire Point to 3,300 fps—snappy stuff! This one's on the comeback trail, and as mentioned previously, they're currently available in easy toting rifles, the Model 70 Featherweight and the short action Model 700 Classic.

257 ROBERTS IMPROVED ACKLEY

This one is simply a blown out 257 Roberts, permitting more case capacity. While the Sierra *RELOADING MANUAL* calls for a 3,000 fps max load with their 100 grain Spitzer in the regular Roberts, that same bullet can be pushed to 3,200 fps (max) in the Improved Ackley.

25/284

As the 6mm/284 is built on the 284 Winchester case by necking down, so is the 25/284. It's a good one and only a gnat's eyelash behind the next cartridge to be discussed. Thus it comes close to being one of the most ideal long rangers. Because of the 284's shorter length, this cartridge can be used in those "short action" bolt guns. It's capable of pushing 100 grain .257 bullets in the 3,300 fps range, and the next one isn't capable of much more.

25/06 REMINGTON

This is **THE** long range varmint cartridge for the average reader and the average varmint hunter, the one who is going to be unwilling to go the custom built rifle route. When it comes to winning wind bucking contests, in combination with super flat trajectory, a hotly loaded 25/06 pushing a sharply pointed 100 grain bullet is going to be tough to beat.

As any reader might expect, the 25/06 is simply the 30/06 necked down. In 1969 Remington standardized the various shoulder angles of 25/06 wildcats that had surfaced since 1920, when A.O. Neider built rifles on it, dubbed the 25 Neider. Factory availability of 25/06 Remington ammo meant plenty of gun manufacturers would begin offering it—and they did. A casual glance through the latest *GUN DIGEST* will confirm more than a dozen makers offering the 25/06.

This load is best suited to extra long range work, where heavy barrel rifles sit the rest steadier, where perfect trigger let offs become a tad easier. Over the counter guns to consider are the Remington 700 BDL Varmint and the Ruger 77 Varmint. Ruger also offers the 25/06 in their Number One Single Shot. One of the very best considerations would be a special order to Remington—for a 26/06 heavy stainless steel barrel version of their 40-X.

The 25/06 is also an outstanding consideration for those who want to make up a custom rifle, especially one that's on the heavy side. If you can hunt where you don't have to carry the gun far from the vehicle, one that weighs thirteen to seventeen pounds will be capable of better results than one that weighs nine. Of course I'm only speaking of extra long range work, like 400, 450, 500, even 550 yards.

While the 25/06 has been around for about fifty years, it didn't achieve its potential until after 4831 became available from Hodgdons after WW II. With this ultra slow burning powder, the 25/06 found its niche. Today's IMR 4831 is good, but it's not as slow as Hodgdons, so you have to drop back about two grains when using IMR's.

Today brass is easily obtained, but military brass was formerly used, merely shoving it through a 25/06 full length resizing die, removing the crimp in the primer pocket, trimming the outside of the neck, and starting to load up. If you can find a buy on 30/06 brass, you can still do that! There'll never be a better long range varmint cartridge than the 25/06, at least one that's available to the average varmint hunter, and available in so many over-the-counter chuck and dog getters.

257 WEATHERBY MAGNUM

This one digests even bigger charges of 4831 than the 25/06, but doesn't gain that much more in velocity. Still, it does outdo that favorite of mine. Yet a bunch of brass'll cost you half the price of a good 25/06 rifle. Barrel life isn't famous in the 257 Weatherby, either. You'll find this cartridge more appropriate on soft skinned big game than on varmints.

The case is a necked down 300 H&H Mag., with the common Weatherby belt. If you have one, take it varmint hunting. If you don't, a 25/06 will serve you better at much less cost.

264 WINCHESTER

As we move from calibers larger than .257 in diameter, we begin to move out of the realm of the true varmint cartridge. However the 264 Winchester could be one of the best long range varmint getters. Based on the 458 Winchester case, the 264 is best with 100 and 120 grain bullets and slow burning powders. Unfortunately the reputation for barrel life is not so good.

6.5 REMINGTON MAGNUM

This one wasn't originally designed with the varmint hunter in mind, but it is fine for the job if 100 grain bullets are chosen, maybe 120's. It's better suited to big game hunting and short action guns. The Model 600 and 660, in which it was originally introduced, have been discontinued.

6.5 × 57

A number of cartridges besides the venerable 7 × 57 Mauser have been necked up and down to 6.5 caliber, but the fact is, other more easily available cartridges do the job better—perhaps with one exception—thus the...

6.5/06

While the 25/06 is my favorite because of easy availability, the 6.5/06 is no slouch. If wind bucking power is your desire, try the 120 grain 6.5 bullet with a hotly loaded 6.5/06. Bob Cassidy, mentioned often in this book, does extremely well with his. Keep in mind that it's possible to use the 270 Winchester case as well as the 30/06 case when necking down to .257 or .264 (6.5mm). Be sure to use caution to measure all cases afterward, especially the necked down 270's, for they be too long. It's also essential to trim the outside of the case necks. Perhaps the ultimate 6.5 would be the 6.5/300 Weatherby, but, as is the case with all Weatherby cases, the price is tremendous compared to 25/06, 270 or especially surplus 30/06 brass. Long live the 30/06!

270 WINCHESTER

While this is the cartridge Jack O'Connor made famous on his big game hunts, it can also be excellent in the varmint field. Handloads with various 100 and 110 grain bullets shoot superbly. Unfortunately only one heavy barrel varmint type rifle is available, and the barrel is only 22 inches long. Anyone with a 270 in his rack for fall and winter big game hunting might as well enjoy the occasional summer go at chucks, prairie dogs and crows with that same gun.

270 WEATHERBY

This one steps bullets along even faster than the regular 270 Winchester, but it was never intended for varmint hunting. Still, if you have one, you might see that it gets some summer duty.

248 WINCHESTER

Reloaders might try the Sierra 120 Spitzer, the Speer 115 grain Hollow Point or the Hornady 120 grain Spire Point if they're bent on varmint hunting with a 284, a cartridge much better suited to big game.

7mm-08

Ditto for the new 7mm-08. It's fine if you want to take your big game rifle on a chuck hunt with proper bullets for the job, but this is big game ordinance.

.308 WINCHESTER

Ditto again for the .308. Try the Speer 110 grain Spire Point, their 130 grain Hollow Point, the Sierra 110 grain Hollow Point, their 125 grain Spitzer, the Hornady 110 grain Spire Point or their 130 Spire Point.

30/06

It's fitting that the 30/06 should be last on this list. If any cartridge ever deserved a medal for worth, this is it. The same bullets suggested for the .308 will work on varmints in the 30/06. Interestingly, both the .308 and 30/06 are available in the excellent Remington 40-XB Rangemaster, a gun that isn't seen often in the summer fields, but the chucks, prairie dogs and crows are certainly glad of that.

FACTORY LOADED CARTRIDGES FOR VARMINT HUNTERS

Following is a listing of factory loaded cartridges available from the three most prominent sources of commercial ammo—Winchester, Remington and Federal:

VARMINT LOADS FROM WINCHESTER

218 Bee	46 gr. OPE	2760
22 Hornet	45 gr. SP	2690
22 Hornet	46 gr. OPE	2690
22-250 Rem.	55 gr. PSP	3730
222 Rem.	50 gr. PSP	3140
223 Rem.	55 gr. PSP	3240
225 Win.	55 gr. PSP	3570
243 Win.	80 gr. PSP	3350
6mm Rem.	80 gr. PSP	3440
25/06 Rem.	90 gr. PEP	3010
250 Sav.	87 gr. PSP	3030
257 Roberts	87 gr. PSP	3170
264 Win.	100 gr. PSP	3320
270 Win.	100 gr. PSP	3480
7mm Rem. Mag.	125 gr. PP	3310
30/06	110 gr. PSP	3380
308 Win.	110 gr. PSP	3180

VARMINT LOADS FROM FEDERAL—PREMIUM— USING SIERRA BOAT-TAIL BULLETS

22-250 Rem.	55 gr. bt tl hp	3730
243 Win.	85 gr. bt tl	3320

VARMINT LOADS FROM FEDERAL—HI-POWER

222 Rem.	50 gr. sp	3140
22-250 Rem.	55 gr. sp	3730
223 Rem.	55 gr. sp.	3240
6mm Rem.	80 gr. sp	3470
243 Win.	80 gr. sp	3350
25/06 Rem.	90 gr. hp	3440

VARMINT LOADS FROM REMINGTON

17 Rem.	25 gr. hp	4040
22 Hornet	45 gr. sp	2690
22 Hornet	45 gr. hp	2690
222 Rem.	50 gr. sp	3140

222 Rem.	50 gr. hp	3140
222 Rem.	55 gr. metal case	3000
222 Rem. Mag.	55 gr. pt sp	3240
222 Rem. Mag.	55 gr. hp	3240
223 Rem.	55 gr pt sp	3240
223 Rem.	55 gr. hp	3240
22-250 Rem.	55 gr. pt sp	3730
22-250 Rem.	55 gr. hp	3730
243 Win.	80 gr. pt sp	3350
243 Win.	80 gr. hp	3350
6mm Rem.	80 gr. pt sp	3470
6mm Rem.	80 gr. hp	3470
6mm Rem.	90 gr. pt spt	3190
250 Sav.	100 gr. pt sp	2820
25/06 Rem.	87 gr. hp	3440
25/06 Rem.	100 gr. pt sp	3230
264 Win.	100 gr. pt sp	3320
270 Win.	100 gr. pt sp	3480
308 Accelerator	55 gr. pt sp	3770
30/06 Accelerator	55 gr. pt sp	4080
30/06	125 gr. pt sp	3140

PROPER BULLETS

Virtually all the bullets in the .224 realm are suitable for varmint hunting. The 40 and 45 grain .224 bullets from most manufacturers are not designed for super high velocity. They're more for the "slower steppers." Sierra offers 40 and 45 grain .223 diameter bullets. There are a few rifles and a few cartridges that require these slightly smaller bullets. Use the 50 to 55 grain .224 bullets for high velocity 22 centerfires, otherwise you might experience bullet breakup or key hole problems on the target.

Following is a listing of excellent *varmint* bullets from today's four most prominent manufactures: Sierra, Speer, Nosler, and Hornady.

6mm—Sierra
  60 grain hp
  70 grain hp
  75 grain hp
  85 grain Spitzer
  85 grain hp bt

Hornady
  70 grain Spire pt.
  75 grain hp.
  87 grain Spire pt.

Speer
75 grain hp
80 grain Spitzer
90 grain Spitzer

25 cal.—Speer
87 grain Spitzer
100 grain hp
100 grain Spitzer
120 grain Spitzer

Sierra
75 grain hp
87 grain Spitzer
90 grain hp bt
100 grain Spitzer
117 grain Spitzer bt
120 grain hp bt

6.5 mm (.264) Sierra
85 grain hp
100 grain hp
120 grain Spitzer

Speer
87 grain hp
87 grain Spitzer
100 grain hp
120 grain Spitzer

270 cal. Speer
100 grain hp
100 grain Spitzer
130 grain Spitzer

Sierra
90 grain hp
110 grain Spitzer
130 grain Spitzer bt
130 grain Spitzer

284 cal. Sierra
120 grain Spitzer

Speer
115 grain hp

Nosler
70 grain hp
70 grain hp match
85 grain Spitz

Hornady
75 grain hp
87 grain Spire pt.
100 grain Spire pt.
120 grain hp

Nosler
100 grain Spitz
120 grain Spitz

Hornady
100 grain Spire pt.
129 grain Spire pt.

Nosler
120 grain Spitz

Hornady
100 grain Spire pt.
110 grain hp
130 grain Spire pt.

Nosler
100 grain Spitz
130 grain Spitz

Hornady
120 grain Spire pt.

30 cal. Speer
   110 grain Spire pt.
   130 grain hp
   Hornady
   110 grain Spire pt.

Sierra
110 grain hp
125 grain Spitzer

CHAPTER 6

Varmint Rifle Accuracy

Varmint rifle accuracy can't be compared to that needed by competitive bench rest shooters. The latter must continually produce one hole groups, and ones that aren't very ragged at that. A varmint rifle that fires one inch groups at one hundred yards and two inch groups at two hundred yards is acceptable, though finer accuracy is desirable. Groups that measure ½ minute of angle are possible from finely tuned varmint rifles, but they can only be expected if that rifle has gone through some refinements, and if reloading and shooting techniques are refined as well. While the accuracy suggestions here will help you fire smaller groups, and also improve your shooting percentages on long range varmints, this chapter is not intended for bench resters. Varmint hunters can learn a great deal from the bench rest clan.

Repeatedly going through the same procedures while shooting is one of the most important ways to reduce rifle group size. This chapter will zero in on a number of factors that contribute to smaller groups. If you fired a group that didn't quite satisfy you yesterday or last week, pay attention to the details of this chapter. I believe you'll be able to fire another test group from the same rifle and do significantly better.

To avoid a hodge podge of accuracy suggestions, they will be separated into three categories: (1) refinements in the rifle rig, (2) refinements in reloads, (3) refinements in shooting technique.

Note wide, flat fore-end of the author's Remington 40-XB 25-06. Note also the Hoppe's leather fore-end bag and Hoppe's adjustable rest. All three factors contribute to fine accuracy.

REFINEMENTS IN THE RIFLE RIG

How the rifle is bedded is perhaps the most important of all aspects contributing to fine accuracy. Suggestions have been touched upon in other chapters. Today glass bedding is the way to go. If you have a used or factory varmint rifle that isn't shooting as accurately as you'd like it to shoot, and it isn't glass bedded already, by all means consider doing so. Glass bedding can be done by following directions supplied with the kits. If you feel someone more experienced can do it better, there are a number of such people. Ask around.

Perfect glass bedding at the recoil lug, around the recoil lug, and for the first few inches of the barrel base are paramount to future accuracy success. Almost equal in importance is perfect bedding all around the action's rear tang. The basic concept behind perfect bedding is to have the rifle recoiling straight back, but striking equally from one side of the recoil lug to the other, and striking equally all around the rear tang. This equality means the action isn't also in a twist. The varmint action can be stiffened to minimize this twist through the use of a one piece scope mount such as the Redfield Junior or one piece scope mounts from a couple of other manufacturers. One piece stiffeners that bridge the action are also made for target type scopes with external adjustments. If your action has a magazine, you might consider having a plate welded across the top of the magazine to make it a single shot. Welding a plate in this position will stiffen the action.

Another reason for your current varmint outfit not performing to the standards you'd prefer can be a well eroded throat—the barrel area immediately forward of the chamber. This could be particularly true of a used varmint outfit you bought, one you had no idea how many shots its former owner or owners had put through it. Once barrel throat erosion takes place, accuracy can be significantly affected. Merely have a good gunsmith, preferably one who is a serious shooter, cut off the barrel threads, rechamber and rethread. You're back in business with a rifle that's as good as new, assuming it was a good shooter when it was new!

A heavier barrel tends to shoot smaller groups than a lighter one. Heavier barrels vibrate more consistently, are less affected by heating, plus the added weight means they sit on the sand bags with more stability. If you're thinking about a new gun or having your current varmintmaster rebarreled, it's worth considering the purchase of a barrel heavier than the whippy job currently adorning your sorry sucker that won't keep good bullets in two inch groups.

A top quality scope sight will naturally help you attain better accuracy. This is particularly true under certain field conditions. In the afternoon I find a great deal of my shooting takes place *into* a setting sun. Here a scope with questionable optics, and/or one with questionable coating on the lenses, isn't worth the powder to blow it sky high. The message— if you're interested in less than minute of angle accuracy—be willing to pay top dollar for one of the scope sights recognized for its fine qualities.

In mounting—tightening down the screws for the rings and some-times for the bases—it's possible to put the scope in a slight twist. A scope so tightened won't shoot consistently. Tighten screws alternately, keeping pressure about the same. Don't tighten one screw to its max-imum, then start tightening the others.

Parallex adjustment is critical when trying to fire the smallest possible groups.

All scopes used for long range varminting need a parallax adjustment on the objective lens. Use that adjustment religiously, whether in the field or at the bench. If you're firing at a known one hundred yard range, don't assume that the hundred yard mark on the objective lens removes all the parallax at one hundred yards. Check to make certain. Get the rifle rig stable on the bags, then move your head up and down and to both sides, still keeping the crosswires in view. If the crosswires move in relationship to the target, the parallax has not been removed. Adjust the objective lens until the parallax is gone—then start your attempt at small group firing.

A crisp, light trigger is best for consistency. There's less chance for the shooter to make an error during the squeeze since that squeeze naturally takes less time. If your current varmint getter is shooting 1¼ inch groups with a factory trigger, there's a good chance you'll reduce most of your future groups to under an inch if you purchase a high quality trigger that's capable of safe adjustment to around a one pound pull.

I love trigger shoes, but not everybody does. A trigger shoe is just that, a wide shoe that fits over the trigger itself. The result is a much broader bearing surface on which to pull against. The lighter the trigger pull, the less important a trigger shoe is, but the converse is also certainly true. If you have a factory trigger on your varmint gun, and you're unwilling to go the route for a quality adjustable trigger, consider investing the couple of bucks it'll take for a trigger shoe. This little tool will make your trigger feel more even, and the pulls will feel lighter than they actually are.

REFINEMENTS IN RELOADS

For big game hunting it's a good idea to full length size your cases to be reloaded. This means easier feeding from the magazine into the chamber, less chance for jamming or encountering that unusually tight

A trigger shoe can contribute to smaller groups, especially if the trigger requires a four-pound pull or more.

round which the bolt won't close down on. Don't forget that shells are almost always loaded singly for varmint hunting, and the gun is only loaded after the quarry has been sighted. When one minute of angle accuracy, or less, is desired, it pays to neck size only. A case that fills the chamber will fire bullets with less velocity variability than the case which fits in a sloppy manner. To make certain they fit all chambers, factory loads must necessarily fit loosely. When shooting for a small group at the bench, do such testing with cases that have been fired previously, and with cases that you've neck sized only.

After neck sizing and primer removal, clean out the primer pockets with the inexpensive and effective tools marketed for this purpose. Cleaning out the primer pocket helps insure that each primer will be seated to the same depth, a factor bench rest bugs have proved important to accuracy. Bench resters also test each case for flash hole size. If one flash hole is appreciably larger than another, you can't expect velocities to be similar. This is one reloading procedure the average varmint hunter may not want to go through, but if you're interested in producing ¾ or ½ minute angle groups from your varmint rifle, it's one you'd better go through. Segregate your cases as to primer hole size.

Reaming the inside of case necks was once popular—this to make necks concentric. This practice has fallen from favor. Instead, the outside necks are often reamed slightly. The ideal is to ream the outside neck so it's .001 to .002 inch smaller than the neck in the rifle's chamber. If every neck you chamber is the same, velocity levels remain more constant from shot to shot.

While bench resters are not interested in maximum velocities, long range varmint hunters must be. This is due to the extreme importance of flat trajectory. The flatter the bullet's path the more the shooter's

Cleaning primer pockets contributes to "one hole" accuracy.

error can be with regard to range estimation, and the less the holdover with relation to the crosswire at the distant ranges. Bench rest shooters tend to choose powders that fill their case, for this practice tends to result in better velocity uniformity. Varminters should do likewise, but with powders that produce the highest velocities—within safe limits, of course. Not only will many full powder case combinations result in less velocity variability, in most varmint cartridges it will also result in maximum velocity. Remember, go strictly by reloading manual recommendations.

Select bullets that are known for their accuracy potential. In .224 caliber there are a number noted for this quality. Some are even called "bench rest" bullets. There are a few of these in 6mm caliber, many in .308 caliber, few in between.

Seating the bullet straight into the case is extremely important for top notch accuracy. One way to get straight seating started is to chamfer the inside of the case neck with the tool used for inside and outside neck deburring (after case trimming). A seater that helps the bullet go into the case neck straight, like the Bonanza Co-Ax Bench Rest Rifle Dies, also helps.

Since you'll be shooting the true varmint rifle in a single shot capacity, don't worry about cartridges being too long for your gun's magazine. Seat your bullets minimally, so they're not quite touching the barrel's lands, but not so far out that a bullet might pull out if you open the bolt in an unfired cartridge. The less "jump" for the bullet, from the case neck to the lands, the less variable the velocity. If bullets are seated minimally, chamber pressures will increase. Cut back powder weight on maximum loads.

REFINEMENTS IN SHOOTING TECHNIQUE

Assuming you're shooting a varmint rig that has minimal recoil, hold the rifle minimally, if at all, for greatest accuracy. One problem we varmint hunters have is "scope black out." This black out can be minimized, even eliminated in some super soft recoilers, with a tight grip on the piece. Grip the rig tightly while hunting alone so you can see where your bullet strikes. If hunting with a partner who will spot your shots, scope black out isn't as much of a problem. The basic idea behind touching the rifle as minimally as possible is that there's less chance for body tremor to send the bullet askew.

Most agree that thumb pressure on the stock should be almost or completely nonexistent. Some have a soft trigger hand grip, but it touches the stock uniformly. Others hardly touch the stock or grip with the trigger hand. Some prefer the fleshy part of the finger on the trigger. I prefer my first joint. Some don't let the hand touch the stock

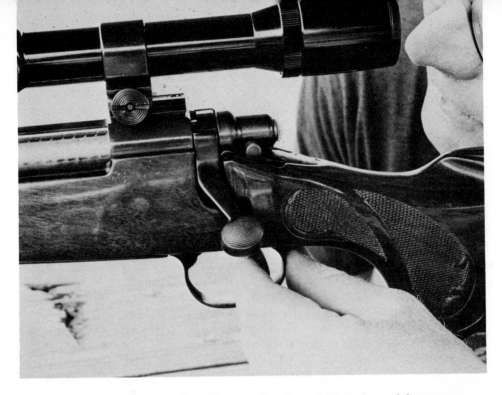

Some who shoot light recoiling rifles keep their face off the stock—and they squeeze the trigger without touching the pistol grip—as shown here.

at all. The thumb is put directly behind the trigger guard, then the trigger finger squeezed against the trigger.

Those of the no-touch-the-stock school keep both their face off the comb and their shoulder off the butt. The idea is "straight-line recoil." Let the rifle come back freely—the same for every shot.

When the rifle to be shot at the bench or at a chuck is placed on the sand bags, place it in such a way that the crosswires are almost perfectly aligned—before you begin to snuggle in for the shot. Getting the rifle perfectly positioned during actual chuck shooting isn't always possible because of the need for some haste. While shooting or attempting to fire small groups from the bench, spend all the time that's necessary getting the rig set perfectly. The ideal is no steering of the gun with the face, the trigger hand or the shoulder.

Steering should come from the left hand, which is placed under the rear portion of the stock, squeezing a malleable sand bag. That steering should ideally be upward only, and the upward steer should be minimal. To review, get the varmint rifle perfectly rigged on the sand bags so the crosswires are a few inches above the target. Then, when the malleable sand bag is squeezed slightly, the crosswires are easily zeroed on the target area.

Though I prefer a wide, flat fore-end on the rifle, I don't like a wide, flat sand bag under it. A malleable "U" shaped sand bag will permit the rifle to sit with more stability. That front bag shouldn't be filled to the hilt with sand. A loose fit in that front "U" shaped bag permits the flat rifle fore-end to "sag" beautifully into place.

The rear bag should also be soft to permit relatively easy squeezing. Here a "V" shaped bag is to be preferred. One important tip is to make certain the toe of the butt or the toe of the recoil pad doesn't dig into the bag. The rear sand bag must be forward of this position— so the rifle is permitted to recoil straight back—past the rear sand bag, not hang up on it.

Take one or two deep breaths, leave part of the last one out, hold it, then begin your squeeze. Depending on the weight of the rifle the crosswires should bob minimally, but they will bob. Learn to "call your shots." If you feel the wires were a fraction of an inch high, left, right, low, whatever, call that bit of "offness" in your mind before looking to see where the bullet actually went. The ability to develop this trait will result in better trigger control, fewer shots zipping off toward the target when the crosswires were not perfectly aligned.

Most barrels are free floating these days. In case yours is bedded the full length of the barrel channel, or in case you have pressure from the stock bearing against the barrel end, get in the habit of placing the fore-end on the front sand bag in exactly the same place for every shot. Doing so will permit the barrel to vibrate more consistently.

By now you're hopefully getting the idea that doing the same thing over and over again for each shot is critical to minimal group size. Remember, I'm making suggestions that will help you fire groups of

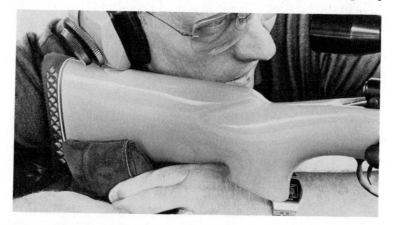

Line up the crosswires so they're only a few inches above the target. Then, touching the stock minimally, if at all, the rear bag is squeezed slightly to bring the crosswires in the scope into proper alignment with the target.

one inch at one hundred yards, perhaps even less. Groups of this size are unlikely unless much attention is paid to the details suggested here.

Finally, a word about cleaning. The first shot out of a clean barrel will seldom go where the remaining bullets will group. There comes a point in varmint shooting where cleaning becomes worthwhile. The smaller the caliber the more often this cleaning should take place. Ralph Hellums, with W.R. Weaver scopes in El Paso, was recently telling me about professional fox hunters in Australia. They opt for the little 17 Remington cartridge and always attempt to shoot the foxes (at night) through the eye. The bullet never comes out. No entrance hole. No exit hole. A perfect pelt for the fur stretcher. Ralph said the key was "....religiously cleaning the little 17 after every 8 shots."

The 22 centerfires can be shot more without small group sizes being affected. Just don't go to the range, fire two boxes of shells getting your scope zeroed, then try to shoot a small group. Go home, clean the barrel, then come back the next day.

I clean my 25-06's after about thirty rounds. Don't fail to use a throat saver in any varmint rifle you have that's capable of centering small groups. Try a patch soaked in Hoppe's #9 first, then soak a properly fitting brush in the same solution. Scrub for six or eight strokes. Follow this with two clean patches previously soaked in Hoppe's #9, then finish with three dry patches. Don't oil the inside of a gun's barrel, especially a fine gun's barrel.

Elbows firmly on the knees permits a steady hold for distance glassing.

CHAPTER 7

Varmint Hunting Binoculars

A pair of binoculars is indispensible for varmint hunting. I wouldn't consider going afield without them. Quality binoculars will make the day afield enjoyable and rewarding. An inferior pair can result in disaster; maybe they'll even make you physically sick.

It's downright dangerous to use the rifle's scope sight to find game. When you're aiming the telescope, you're also aiming the rifle. If looking for game, that has to mean you're pointing the rifle at buildings, farm animals, and occasionally people. Not only is using the scope unsafe for finding woodchucks, the scope is also extremely inefficient. The field of view, even from low power scopes, is simply too small. Scoped rifles are also too heavy for extended use. Binoculars are so much better there's never a need to consider anything else.

Today we have a number of excellent quality binoculars from which to choose, and the price of a good pair is a bargain in today's world of runaway inflation. The makers must have learned a great deal about the how-to of coming up with fine lenses, and about coating them. For two to three hundred dollars you can buy binoculars superior to those of yesteryear, which might have cost more, despite the fact that yesteryear's dollar value was far greater.

Not only has the quality of binoculars improved, their weight has been reduced as well. This is particularly true of prism type binoculars, though I'm not personally sold on the prism variety. I have a pair of 6 × 30 Swarovski's (not prisms) that only weigh eighteen ounces. Bushnell Custom Compacts only weigh eleven ounces. These are a bit light and small for critical work—scanning hayfields all day for chucks.

I've done considerable binocular testing this past year, and I've revamped some of my former opinions. I was once sold on the ten powers, despite their bulk and heft. I am no longer so pleased with them. I'm more convinced than ever that six or seven power is plenty for a hand held glass, or one a varmint shooter supports on sand bags for careful, long term viewing. After testing 33 different pairs of varying powers from eight different manufacturers, I purchased one pair for my personal use—those previously mentioned Swarovski 6 × 30's.

Individual binoculars are a lot like individual cars. Some that come off the assembly line are better than others. Through use and testing one may prove better than its brother. Surely all readers would agree that the same car models differ in many respects. Test fifty different Ford Fairmonts at random, even if they all came off the same assembly line, and you'll find fifty different cars, at least in some respects. Some will wear out engines or transmissions faster. Others will burn more oil than their counterparts after so many miles. Still others may run through brakes in no time at all. Some won't stay in front wheel alignment as long as others. So it is with binoculars.

Therefore look through binoculars critically before you plunk down your hard earned cash. Test pair after pair—all the store will permit you to glass through if possible. Look for qualities like ease of focus, how bright the objects are that you focus on, how clear those objects appear to your eyes. Try reading some printed words through these binoculars. Go back and forth between several pairs. One or two will begin to shine. Depth of field is important. Binoculars with less depth of field have to have the adjustment knob turned slightly every time you glass at a different distance. Binoculars that are in focus from one hundred yards to infinity need little if any focus adjustment at either range. These are what you're looking for.

The size of the objective lens (second number in a binocular's description—i.e., 6 × 30—the 30 means the objective lens is 30mm in diameter) has a great deal to do with how much light goes through the binocular and gets to the eye. Consequently, binoculars with larger objective lenses tend to permit more light—important all day long, but particularly in the late afternoon when light is fading and many chucks are in the long shadows. Trouble is big objective lenses weigh more. More weight can be fatiguing, especially when binoculars are hand held, less so if the binocular is firmly steadied on a tubular sand bag. Bob Cassidy has a fabulous pair of Japanese 7 × 50's, made before, during or just after the Second World War. Though outstanding for their clarity, they do weigh more than my 6 × 30 Swarovskis.

Many will be tempted to buy binoculars of more than seven power. My experience says don't. A good 7 × 35 is tough to beat. The Bushnell and Bausch & Lomb 7 × 35's did extremely well in my tests, and they won't tear your bank account to shreds. A glass of this type is far easier to hand hold with reasonable steadiness compared to a 9X or a 10X binocular. A binocular of less power will also cost less compared to those of more power and comparable quality. You'll also find the field of view in a lower power pair will be significantly bigger, an important factor when scanning fields for chucks, or the prairie for "dogs." While you concentrate on looking hard at the center portion of the field, a good glass makes it easy to see the periphery, and this is where many a chuck is picked up by the discerning eye. High power binoculars don't make it easier to see chucks, they can make it more difficult because of their smaller fields of view.

Whenever possible it's best to hold your binoculars to your eyes in the most stable manner. The best stability I've found is to rest them firmly on a "cylindrical" sand bag. Cut the top and bottom off a bag used for shot, then sew a circular piece of shot bag material on the bottom. Fill full with sand, then tightly hand sew a circular piece of shot bag material on the top. The cylindrical shaped bag sits flat on the car roof, hood, fence post, etc. The binoculars atop it sit flat, too. Get accustomed to viewing with binoculars in this manner and you won't exchange it for any other way.

Carrying a large sand bag like this in the field to rest your binoculars on is certainly out of the question. In this situation the most stable position is to sit down, knees up, then rest the elbows on the knees, your forefingers on your forehead, your thumbs on your cheeks, as the hands grip the binocular. The more distant the area you're trying to view, the more important binocular stability becomes.

Some companies that make suitable binoculars for varmint hunting follow:

Bushnell Optical
2828 Foothill Blvd.
Pasadena, CA 91107

Jason/Empire
9200 Cody
Overland Park, KS 66214

Ziess
444 5th Ave.
New York, NY 10018

Tasco
P.O. Box 520080
Miami, FL 33152

Swarovski
Strieter Corp.
2100 18th Ave.
Rock Island, IL 61201

Swift Instruments
952 Dorchester Ave.
Boston, MA 02125

E. Leitz
Rockleigh, NJ 07647

CHAPTER 8

Distance, Long Range Holdovers and Doping the Wind

Any varmint hunter interested in truly long range shooting is going to be holding over the tiny target in his scope field most of the time. When these long shots are involved the slightest whisper of a breeze is going to blow the bullet well off course. If there's a stiff 20-mile-an-hour crosswind, the effect on the bullet is going to be dramatic. Gusting breezes create the most difficult conditions for precision work by varmint hunters. The difference in trajectory between 150 and 200 yards is negligible. The target appears plenty big enough in the scope, and, as long as a flat shooting cartridge is being used, the difference in trajectory between 150 and 200 yards is less than an inch. However, the difference in trajectory between 500 and 550 yards will be more than a foot for most cartridges. The point is—you can misjudge 150 for 200 yards, or vice versa, and you're still going to kill the chuck you're aiming at. Misjudge 500 for 550, or vice versa, and the bullet doesn't have a chance to encounter chuck flesh. This is fact without even considering how much smaller the target appears in the scope at the longer distances.

Among other problems the precision chuck shooter faces, he must be an accurate judge of distance. Secondly, he must know the exact trajectory of the rifle he's shooting, plus be able to relate that trajectory with the crosswires in his scope. Finally, after taking the first two problems into consideration he then must be able to judge the wind accurately so he can still place his bullet exactly where he wants it to go. It's all this precision that combines to make long range chuck shooting the most challenging sport there is when there's an animal out there at the end of the bullet's flight path.

Judging distance can be a great deal easier if you have golf experience. This is another precision game. Before every shot the player must decide whether he needs a spoon or a brassie, a nine-iron or a wedge, etc. Golfers learn to judge distance because they're forced into doing so for every shot. But golfers are given a great deal of help, too. Their scorecard indicates the exact distance from every tee to every green. Every time a golfer plays a different course he gets to see different distances from every tee, but the exact distances are spelled out for him on the scorecard. Within a relatively short time a new golfer who pays attention learns to judge distance accurately. If this golfer turns chuck hunter, he's going to use his distance judging capabilities to the utmost advantage.

Since I was once an avid golfer, I'm able to make good judgments for distance—by spotting a chuck and thinking carefully, "A good drive, then a six-iron—about 380 yards!" Then the 380 yards goes into my mental computer, conjuring up the trajectory for the pig rifle I'm carrying that particular day, and how that weapon is sighted in. Within seconds I'm wrapped around the stock and have the proper hold.

When extreme distances come into play, say four hundred yards and more, using past experiences with golf to judge distance becomes less and less effective. Experience helps, but some shooters make themselves learn quicker than others. Here's how you can learn to become an excellent judge of distance in a relatively short time. Make yourself estimate the distance to the target *every time* you line up the crosswires on a varmint. Before the season starts, pace off these distances, 200, 250, 300, 350, 400, 450, 500 and 550 yards. Sight your extra long range chuck piece in three inches high at one hundred yards. Next, at each of the distances suggested, fire a three-shot group. This group will tell you everything you need to know about your bullet's trajectory. You'll know exactly where the bullet strikes at each of these distances. Later, in the hunting field, with this information on a piece of paper in your wallet or taped to your rifle's stock, you'll be able to tell whether you've misjudged the distance to the target by overstating or understating, simply by finding out how high or low the bullet struck with relation to your hold.

To summarize, there are two keys to the above. First you must know the exact trajectory of the bullet and load you're shooting. Second, you must estimate the distance prior to every shot, then hold for that estimated distance with your placement of the crosswires—commensurate with your rifle's trajectory.

In an earlier chapter I penned paragraphs about my preference for a scope with two horizontal crosswires. At the extra long ranges a second crosswire under the main crosswire becomes extremely beneficial. The top horizontal wire is used for sighting in, and as the reference point for a great deal of one's shooting. Depending upon cartridge, bullet and load, that could mean using the top wire as the main reference for shooting to four hundred yards or so. Eventually, however, the top wire must be held so far above the target that it becomes increasingly difficult to be precise with it as a reference point. This is when the bottom wire becomes an aid because the chuck target, during the hold, is closer to that bottom wire. Additionally, the precision rifleman will know the difference between his two horizontal wires. If the distance separating the two is 4 inches at 100 yards, it's going to be 8 inches at 200, 12 inches at 300, 16 inches at 400, 20 inches at 500, 24 inches at 600. Not only does that bottom wire give a more precise aiming point, if the first shot has missed and the shooter can accurately judge how far it missed, he combines that knowledge with known cartridge trajectory and the known distance between the wires at the suspected range. Chances are excellent the second shot will come appreciably closer to Mr. Woodchuck.

Lacking a pair of horizontal crosswires, the chuck hunter is going to have to make do with zeroing in exactly on the trajectory of his pet chuck load and making it a point to try and estimate the distance to the target prior to every shot. A partner who calls the misses will be indispensible. Working together like this, two novice hunters can become lethal on woodchucks in a relatively short period of time—assuming they have the proper long range rifles, scopes and loads, and that they work together in the manner suggested. Most will be unwilling to work hard enough. Consequently they won't make appreciable progress.

One of Bob Cassidy's favorite phrases, "accumulated guesswork," can be applied to doping the wind. Others may spend years randomly blasting away at all manner of chucks and never learn much. Conversely, by working hard every minute one is in the chuck field, a great deal can be learned on every outing.

As distance must be judged prior to every shot, so range estimation can become more and more precise. The precision rifleman must also judge wind accurately, and hold for it every time he prepares to pull the trigger. The problem here is that wind can be constantly changing. Once the shooter has the range estimated accurately, he can hold precisely to make a telling or near telling shot time after time. Not so with regard to the wind. At five hundred yards it might blow a 100 grain Sierra, spit from a 25-06 at max velocity, one foot off course the first shot, then the bullet can be caught in a stiffer breeze a half minute later, so the second shot is blown two feet off course.

While the target is in the scope field, the rifleman must be constantly watching the movement of the grass blades. He continually makes slight adjustments in his hold to the waving grass, hoping that when the trigger sends the firing pin on its way that the wind judgment will be as accurate as he can possibly make it.

Previously I suggested getting in the habit of calling each shot taken at the practice range—before looking at the paper target to see exactly where the bullet made its hole. Use this same philosophy with regard to the wind. Try to call your shot with regard to wind estimation prior to hearing your shooting partner tell you where the bullet hit.

Grass blades billowing out where the chuck is feeding are only one part of wind doping. How much the wind is blowing where you and the rifle are located is even more important. This is because a bullet affected by the wind at the beginning of its flight path is going to be much farther off course than one affected by wind near the end of its flight path. Consequently, the wind in the vicinity of the rifle must be taken into consideration before lying down to shoot. How does that breeze feel on your face? Keep the feel of that breeze on your face in mind while sighting and final squeezing. A last second adjustment might be made after feeling a wind change just prior to trigger let-off.

Air currents occasionally come from opposite directions. I've seen the day when the wind was blowing one direction where we shooters were positioned, but the wind was blowing in the opposite direction out at the distant target. These are not only tough wind doping conditions, they are disconcerting ones. I've also seen the day when the wind was blowing from the west by our guns and also out where the chucks were. Unfortunately the wind was blowing east in the valley between us.

If there are variable wind conditions in your favorite hunting field, you might consider tying some type of light flag on stakes at measured distances. This set up will assist you with distance estimation and wind velocity and currents as well.

I wonder if some readers are getting the idea that I'm making too much of a fuss about all of this. My suggestions for precision distance estimation, holdovers, and doping the wind might appear like too many additional complications to some. You must realize that precision shooting **is** complicated, difficult, challenging, and requires both work on the scene and forethought prior to the hunt. Though every reader or varmint hunter might be unwilling to go to great pains to achieve the precision I'm talking about, more and more are finding true satisfaction in this approach. There was a time when the philosophy of varmint hunting was much different than it is today. The idea was to kill as many of the son-of-guns as possible. Today's riflemen don't have a vendetta against woodchucks or prairie dogs, regardless how many of these critters might exist in some areas. Today's riflemen are seeking more precision, more challenge, more difficulty. Becoming a better and better long range shooter is the essence of future varmint hunting. Precision may never be the objective for great multitudes of hunters, but for other thousands it will be the most satisfying sport they encounter all year long.

CHAPTER 9

Rests

No serious woodchuck or prairie dog hunting can be done without some type of rest that helps steady the rifle. There are two primary reasons for this: (1) both chucks and "dogs" are small targets, much smaller than any big game animal, (2) these varmints are taken at relatively long range—consistently.

Consider the other factors involved. As a rifleman becomes more and more interested in chucks or prairie dogs, he tends to favor more precision in his shooting. That means longer and longer shots, an effort to zero in on the animal's head or neck area when possible. For anyone to perform precision work, a firm, steady rest is essential. Few will deny this necessity.

There are all manner of so-called "chuck rests" on the market. When a rifleman attains retirement age, he has time to dream up the idea for what he thinks is the best rifle rest ever made, manufactures a few of them in his garage or basement, then probably claims all his chuck hunts as tax deductible. More power to him!

Trouble is, many of these rests aren't good enough for serious precision work at truly long range, or they're not portable enough for carrying in the field. A rest that's suitable for precision work should be just as suitable for firing small groups at the shooting range. If tested at the shooting range, most chuck rests fail miserably—compared to shooting off sand bags. The rest you think is so great for chuck hunting should be tried under bench conditions. Maybe it'll perform even better than you expected. If it doesn't, you then have good reason to seek out a rest that is suitable, capable of the utmost in precision.

Bob Cassidy's rest idea is the one I use when super long range "chucking" is on the agenda. Using it, lying prone at the rifle range, I can shoot groups as small as I can from the bench. The trouble with Bob's rest is that it isn't portable. Of course the rifles we use for extra long range shooting aren't portable either.

Bob's rest isn't patented or marketed by anyone. The rest is made of micarta, an extremely stiff board used mainly for industrial applications. Micarta comes in ½, ⅜ and ¼ inch thicknesses. The ¼ inch micarta is plenty thick enough, but micarta in any size is tough to find. You might have to substitute ⅜ inch plywood. Two pieces of micarta, approximately eight inches wide and eleven or twelve inches long, are attached via two hinges. With a saw a "U" is formed on the same end where the hinges are attached. On the opposite end of the micarta something sharp is affixed, which acts as legs that won't slip when the rest is planted solidly on the ground.

A smallish and partially filled sand bag is placed on the micarta's "U". The rifle's fore-end sits here. Another sand bag (I like the Hoppe's #3021 Rear Rest Bag) sits on the ground. The rifle's butt portion sits on this bag. It's important that the toe of the stock or recoil pad slides past this sand bag, and that the stock or recoil pad don't dig into the rear sand bag during recoil.

If you're interested in serious extra long range chuck shooting (four hundred, five hundred yards, or more), consider this rest Bob Cassidy has developed. You'll have to make it yourself, for it's not commercially available. By separating the hinge to a greater or lesser degree, you can elevate or lower this rest. It's suitable only for firing from the prone position, but that's the only one suitable for super long range work, lacking a true bench rest.

When concentrating on those extra long range shots, I never get far from the vehicle. Sometimes we drive right into the farmer's fields, but only after seeking permission to do so. If hunting on the move (away from the vehicle), there's no question that my favorite rest is the Harris Bipod. This is the unique rest that ingeniously attaches to the swivel stud on the rifle's fore-end. A swivel stud in the Bipod still permits attaching the sling swivel. This means that the varmint rifle with a Harris Bipod can be slung over the shoulder in the normal manner. There's no rest to carry—both hands are free.

While carrying the Harris Bipod, fold the legs forward toward the end of the barrel; thus they're out of the way when your rifle is over your shoulder. When it's time to shoot, fold the legs down, snapping them into place under spring tension. Each leg is individually adjustable, which makes it possible to keep the rifle resting level even if shooting from uneven terrain. The leg adjustments also make it possible to raise the position of the rifle. This is often necessary because of intervening grass. There are two models. The larger Harris Bipod has legs 12½ inches long and that telescope to 23 inches. With these legs fully extended, you can fire this larger model from the sitting position. I favor the smaller Harris Bipod since it's even lighter. You'll never find one as light (nine ounces), that permits steadier holds. The legs are eight inches long, but they telescope to thirteen inches. Unlike the larger model, the shorter Bipod has intermittent adjustments between eight and thirteen inches. Both are priced in the thirty dollar range. Write Harris Engineering, Barlow, KY 42024, in case your local dealer doesn't supply this item. It's so light you can even use it for big game hunting and never know it's there—in case you encounter big game where any long distance shooting can be expected.

MTM Molded Products Co., Dayton, OH 45414, makes a lightweight plastic "walking stick" that's fine for summer chucking. It carries easily and one could rig an attachment so it would dangle from the belt to leave both hands free. A rest for the rifle's fore-end "cams" up or down on this walking stick so the fore-end can be placed at the proper position. The rifle can be fired prone at the lower settings, while the sitting position is possible at the higher settings. This "walking stick" is excellent also for the handgunner. He can plant the rest securely

Shooting from sitting position with MTM "Walking Stick"

121

in the ground, then rest his weapon on the very top of the walking stick for good stability.

Cravner's Gun Shop, 1627 5th Ave., Ford City, PA 16226, markets a "Micro-Rest" shooting stand. It's adjustable in a number of ways. Another is the Robo Rifle Rest made of durable aluminum castings. You can push it into the ground. Like the Cravner "Micro-Rest," the rifle's butt and fore-end rest on the same plane.

There's no question there are a number of other rests currently available for chuck and prairie dog hunting, and there will undoubtedly be more offered in future years. Nobody denies the need for a firm steady rest when long distance work at smallish targets is in the offing. The right rest will permit you to enjoy perfect let offs when a chuck or dog is locked in your scope's crosswires.

Cravner rifle rest.

CHAPTER 10

Hunting Prairie Dogs

Prairie dog hunting was once extremely popular, but a multitude of shooters were lost when state, federal and local agencies declared full scale war on this tiny varmint. Prairie dogs were poisoned in wholesale numbers. Old time "dog" hunters didn't find the high volume, long distance rifle sport they once knew, so many gave up. Happily, the prairie dog has been making a comeback of late. A bureaucratic war is still declared on this furry little critter, but the battle isn't as intense as in the past. On a one, two or three day prairie dog hunt, a fella can now get as much live game rifle experience as an enthusiastic and well heeled big game hunter can acquire in a lifetime. Here's a varmint hunting sport where a rifleman can learn a tremendous amount about his rifle, doping the wind, estimating distance, holdovers, trajectories, experiment with different calibers and cartridges and a whole lot more. All this beneficial experience can come in a very short period if one devotes himself to gunning prairie dogs.

There are two species of prairie dogs, the black-tailed and the white-tailed. Though riflemen do shoot both, it's the black prairie dog that gets the most attention—by far. The white-tailed is more a creature of the eastern Rocky Mountain foothills, while the black-tailed lives on the true flat land prairie or rolling grassland prairie. The hot bed of prairie dog hunting takes place in western South Dakota, southwestern North Dakota, eastern and central Montana, eastern Colorado and Wyoming, western Nebraska, and Kansas.

Anyone who has never seen a prairie dog town will find the written descriptions hard to believe. I've seen dog towns in South Dakota's

123

The prairie dog. No live rifle target is so abundant and offers so much volume shooting.

Buffalo Gap National Grasslands that were so big I couldn't see from one end to the other, even from a high vantage point on a crystal clear day. Some towns stretch for miles in length across the barren prairie, but many are also several miles wide. There are thousands upon thousands of prairie dogs in towns this size. They oughta call 'em prairie dog cities.

Once one takes up a shooting position, there may be literally hundreds of prairie dogs within view. I found such numbers hard to believe, until I saw it myself. The more times you fire your rifle, the more prairie dogs there will be that become wary. The noise'll spook 'em into their holes. It may take five shots or fifty but eventually you'll have to move on to a new shooting position. That move will never have to be far—one, two, three hundred yards, settle into a comfortable position again and start shooting. Find a big dog town and you can keep shooting and moving like this all day long—and you'll only be able to cover a very small portion of the town.

Like long range woodchuck hunting, prairie dog sport is not one for lone shooters. You'll gain the most benefit from dog hunting experiences if you do it in the company of a shooting buddy or two. No matter what rifle caliber you're using, there's a good chance you'll "black out" in the scope when the rifle recoils. Consequently, it's almost impossible to determine where your bullet strikes. By having a buddy alongside with binoculars, you can have each shot placement called for you.

Let's say you make a range and wind estimation, place the crosswires accordingly, carefully squeeze the trigger, then black out. The bullet misses, but where? High? Low? Right? Left? A combination of high right? Or low left? Your buddy calls the shot immediately, "about three inches high, four or five inches left." When he calls your shots, you learn something. Did you over or underestimate the distance? Did the wind blow the bullet more or less than you expected? By continually repeating experiences like these, a rifleman can really begin to learn something about range estimation and wind doping, two factors that will contribute significantly to a person's capabilities with a rifle in his hands. In addition to the enjoyment and satisfaction any reader will get from prairie dog hunting, that person will also come away from every hunt of several days a much wiser and more capable rifleman—no matter what the next game might be that he gets in his scope sight.

On my first prairie dog hunt in South Dakota, a game protector who was showing Bob Bell and me a few of the many dog towns in his bailiwick told us that a week or so previous to our hunt a party from Minnesota had come out, five dog hunters strong. In less than a week of hunting, this group fired all the five thousand shells that they brought along. Let's say you were one of the five. How could you help but learn a great deal about rifle shooting if you fired a thousand rounds at game?

How many rifles should you bring on a prairie dog hunt? On my first trip I lugged seven. Since then I've pared down the arsenal a bit, but it still pays to take several. You never know when a rig is going to break down—for any one of a thousand reasons. Best to have ample backup. Enough loaded cartridges is a similar problem. If you have to travel any distance to your dog hunting, you should have plenty of ammo on hand. Running out the second or third day of a week long trip would certainly put a damper on the outing. The idea then should be to take far more ammunition than you think you'll ever need. For a week's trip I'd never consider leaving home with less than a thousand rounds.

Any cartridge will do for prairie dog hunting, but I feel two of the very best are the 222 and 223 Remington, the latter being the same brass case that the military is now using. This brass is consequently readily available and cost is reasonable. A recent advertisement from Godfrey Reloading Supply (Box 688, City Limits Rd., Brighton, IL 62012) says commercial 223 fired brass was five dollars per hundred, fifty dollars per thousand. Military 223 brass is even cheaper. I assume these

Bob Bell levels on a distant prairie dog with 788 Remington in 223 caliber, ideal for prairie dogs.

have the crimped primer pocket—which can be reamed out by hand or with a power drill properly rigged. An ad I checked in the *Shotgun News* (Homer Cleckler, 3774 Spring Dr., Huntsville, TX 77340) showed military brass for only fifteen dollars per thousand.

The 222 and 223 are sorta ballistical twins. If I were going out to buy one today I'd lean toward the 223 because of the ready availability of lower priced brass casings. Remington makes two outstanding rifles for prairie dog consideration. For the hunter on the move, there's the no frills Model 788 bolt action. This gun has an excellent trigger, is extremely low priced, represents outstanding value, and 788's, especially in 223 Rem. caliber, shoot like crazy. Seemingly the gun and the cartridge were made for one another. While the other calibers in the 788 line are short 18½ inchers intended for use on big game, the 223 (and the 22-250) sport twenty-four inch barrels. All the steadier for holding those crosswires on something furry like a prairie dog at about 225 yards!

The second outstanding 223 caliber rifle from Remington is their Model 700 Varmint. This one carries a heavy barrel, ⅝ inch in diameter near the muzzle. The 700 Varmint Model would be the top choice for the prairie dog hunter shooting from his vehicle where carrying is no consideration. With a 10X scope you can expect the 700 Varmint to tote over ten pounds. The 788, similarly scoped, will weigh approximately two pounds less. This gun'll be ideal for carrying across the prairie, say with a Harris Bipod attached to the front swivel stud.

There are a couple of other 223 considerations. The Savage 340 comes in 223 Remington and costs fifteen to forty dollars less than the 788. The 340 unfortunately doesn't have a trigger that can compare with the 788, and it doesn't have the accuracy reputation of the Remington. The 340 also comes in 22 Hornet and 222 Remington.

The great Sako Sporter comes in 223, but it wears a price tag almost triple the 788. Still, the Sako is an excellent value. It also comes in 17 Rem., 222 Rem., 22-250, 220 Swift, 243 Win., 25-06 and a host of other calibers. Don't sell the Sako Sporter short, but be willing to part with a great deal of do-re-mi when you walk into the store intending to take one home.

From Ruger there's the Number Three Carbine Single Shot in 223 (also 22 Hornet). This little six pounder with twenty-two inch barrel has an adjustable trigger. Frankly, I've never shot a Number Three (love those Ruger Number Ones though), but this one would be worth considering.

The 222 Remington is available in several rifles—all those previously mentioned (except the Ruger Number Three), plus the following: BSA CF-2, Remington 700 ADL and BDL and the 788.

The 222 Rem. Mag. has lost its popularity with the prominence of the 223. These two are almost dead ringers ballistically, though the

127

case is different. Remington's factory loaded 55 grain soft point 222 Rem. Magnum's muzzle velocity is the same as the 223's 55 grain soft point—3240 fps. The regular 222's muzzle velocity with the 50 grain soft point is 3140 fps—which I call a very close second. No current, common rifle is chambered for the 222 Remington Magnum, though many previous ones were. The cartridge is still readily available in guns from custom smiths. If you have a 222 Remington Magnum in your gun rack, it's ideally suited to dog hunting. If you don't have one, choose either the 222 or 223. As previously suggested, lean toward the 223 because of the easy accessibility of inexpensive brass.

The handloader will find either the standard 222 or the newer 223 an easy one to work with. Both take the small rifle primer. I suggest the Remington 7½, which was made to order for these two cartridges. Any .224 caliber bullet will do the job on a prairie dog, but I suggest three from Sierra—their 50 grain "Blitz," 52 grain Hollow Point Boattail Bench Rest or 52 Grain Hollow Point Bench Rest. All four of these bullets will open very well, plus give exceptional accuracy in the 222 or 223 Remington. DuPont's 4198 is an excellent powder choice for either of these cartridges. Twenty grains of 4198 will drive the 50 grain bullet in the 222 to 3100 fps. Twenty and a half grains of 4198 is the maximum load, giving 3200 fps in the 50 grain bullet from the 222. For the 52 and 53 grain bullets try 19.8 grains of 4198 for 3000 fps in the 222, 20.4 grains being the max for this bullet size, resulting in 3100 fps. In the 223, 21.4 grains of 4198 gives the 50 grain bullet 3100 fps, while 22 grains of 4198 is the max 223/4198 load, resulting in 3200 fps. With the 52 and 53 grain bullets in the 223 try 20.6 grains of 4198 for 3000 fps., while the max load is 21.2 grains of 4198 for 3100 fps. Note that in these small cases a minute additional powder charge results in considerably more velocity. Similarly, a small increase in the powder charge also results in considerably more chamber pressure. Don't put too much powder in the 222, 223 (or any other case for that matter) or you can expect drastic results. Be extremely careful weighing powder charges.

The 222 and 223 aren't the only cartridges one can use for prairie dogs. I've used many others, and these critters have probably been killed with everything from a 22 short to a 300 Weatherby. The main reason I claim the 223 is so ideal is the inexpensive brass, contingent with minimal recoil. Recoil in most any cartridge recommended for varmint hunting is never a problem—until it comes to the high volume shooting which can be experienced on almost every prairie dog outing. Two shooters probably wouldn't fire more than about thirty shots each day on an outstanding woodchuck hunt. Prairie dog hunters might shoot that many times in an hour—or possibly even more frequently! That repetitive firing will eventually cause recoil to get to anyone. The multiple slight jolt to the face and shoulder eventually gets to shooters, but perhaps the noise of the muzzle blast is equally important. The 222 and 223 have a reasonably mild report, much milder than a 22-250, 220 Swift or cartridges of larger caliber.

What about other cartridge possibilities for prairie dogs? I love the little 17 Remington. I always pack this one for my prairie dog hunts. The report is even milder than the 222 or 223. Lesser kick as well. My handloads step the 25 grain Remington hollow points along at about 3750 fps. There's more than enough energy to knock the socks off a prairie dog to about 225, maybe 250 yards, the max effective range of this cartridge. DuPont's 4198 is also an ideal powder for the 17. Try 19.1 grains for 3800 fps with the 25 grain hollow point. I have about 200 casings for the 17, so I always use it for one or two days on my prairie dog trips.

All rifles should be cleaned regularly. Don't expect to fire a thousand rounds at prairie dogs with one rifle and not clean it all week. Accuracy from such an unclean barrel won't be worth a hoot. A dirty 17 barrel is particularly prone to accuracy drop off. Be ready to run a solvent soaked patch through a 17 every time you return to the vehicle if you're walking up your dogs, every couple of boxes of ammo fired if you're shooting from or close to your vehicle. Follow up the powder solvent soaked patch with a dry one. Each evening, back at the motel, give every gun you've used that day a thorough cleaning—solvent, brass brushing, the works. Taylor and Robbins (Box 164, Rixford, PA 16745) makes a jig (Throat Saver) and cleaning rod for virtually all rifles that will prevent throat erosion, always a problem associated with using a cleaning rod. The newer plastic throat savers might not hold up for several lifetimes like the Taylor and Robbins, but they're

The plastic "bore saver" from MTM Plastics. Due to the great amount of shooting being done on a prairie dog hunt, regular bore cleaning is suggested. This "bore saver" prevents premature barrel throat erosion.

less expensive. In pushing through a tight fitting patch with a rod, or a brass brush soaked in Hoppe's, the rod continually scrapes the throat of the barrel bore. As this part of the barrel wears away, accuracy drops off—and it doesn't take much wear before a noticeable drop off in accuracy occurs. The Taylor and Robbins Throat Saver (and the newer plastic ones), which fits snugly into the action like the rifle's bolt, has a hole into which the cleaning rod is inserted. This jig holds the cleaning rod firmly, preventing it from bending inside the barrel and thus scraping the throat area. Varmint hunters serious about accuracy shouldn't be without some type of throat saver.

Some of the varmint cartridges of many years ago continue to be ideal. The 22 Hornet is still produced in the Ruger Number Three and the Savage 340. This cartridge is capable of driving 50 grain bullets at 2800 fps if Winchester 296 is used. The max load is 12.2 grains. Work up to this max load slowly. The 218 Bee, introduced way back in 1938, is capable of similar velocities with 4198 and the 50 grain bullet. The 219 Donaldson Wasp came on the varmint scene around 1941. It's capable of driving 50 grain .224 bullets to 3500, even 3600 fps. The 219 Zipper was born four years earlier. Using a rimmed case like the Wasp, it spit out 50 grainers at similar velocities. The Bee, Wasp and Zipper were all popular cartridges normally built on single shot, falling block actions.

The 225 Winchester, a very good varmint cartridge, may be doomed into oblivion. No common arms manufacturer is currently offering a rifle in this caliber. It's capable of driving 50 grain bullets in the 3700 and 3800 fps realm. The 224 Weatherby Magnum can average another 100 fps over the 225 Winchester, and this is an excellent cartridge, though I believe all these, save the 222 Rem., 223 Rem., 22 Hornet and 218 Bee, have too much recoil for serious, repetitive prairie dog shooting.

While many consider the ultimate woodchuck rifles to be the 22-250 Varminter and the 220 Swift, they belt my shoulder too much and make too much noise if I'm going to be firing one hundred to three hundred rounds per day on my typical prairie dog trips. The 22-250 was originally based on the 250-3000 case. Like the 224 Weatherby, it will spew out those 50 grain .224 bullets at 3800 to 3900 fps. The 220 Swift, introduced way back in 1935, gives similar velocities. Though more powder can be added to the Swift in most cases, compared to the Varminter, only little additional velocities can be obtained. If they are attained, a drop off in accuracy could result. Accuracy with both cartridges is often at its peak when using 4064 and obtaining velocities of around 3800 fps, maybe a tad over.

I don't consider the 243 Win. and 6mm Rem. ideal for work on prairie dogs, but many are used. Plenty of .243 diameter bullets go zipping across the prairies every summer. One benefit of these cartridges is that there are so many different rifles currently available that offer one or both.

The list of cartridge possibilities could go on for pages, but enough is enough. What about how to hunt prairie dogs? My favorite way to hunt them is on the move, with a light bolt rifle and one hunting companion. We alternate shooting and calling shots. I might fire five rounds while my buddy glasses through binoculars to determine where my bullets are hitting, in case they happen to miss the dog I'm holding on slightly. Then we switch roles.

The 223 Remington 788 is a personal favorite for this type of shooting. Rigged with a Weaver 10X scope, heat waves coming off the hot and bright prairie won't be too objectionable. I like to attach the Harris Bipod (Harris Engineering, Barlow, KY 42024). These come in two sizes. I prefer the smaller one because I do all my shooting from the prone position. The larger Harris Bipod is more suited to use from the sitting position. The Bipod legs are individually adjustable, important when you're firing from uneven ground. With my left hand squeezing the butt of the rifle for minor up and down and side to side adjustments in the hold, it's surprising how steady one can learn to hold a rifle with the Harris Bipod attached. This Bipod is ingeniously made to fit into the front swivel stud of the rifle. A screw adjustment (coin slotted) makes it possible to snug the rest up very tight with the fore-end. It can be removed and attached to another rifle in less than a minute. The Harris Bipod is also rigged with its own swivel stud. You merely attach your detachable rifle sling to this stud and slip the sling, rifle with Bipod attached, over your shoulder. The Bipod adds less than a pound of additional weight, but permits precision shooting to over 250 yards.

My 17 Remington on the Model 700 action, BDL version, is also excellent for walk up prairie dog hunting. A heavy barreled Varmint rifle like the 700 Varmint in 223 is, to my mind, a bit heavy for this work, though I've used one. The 17 and Model 788 in 223 simply are better suited to on-the-move hunting.

As mentioned previously, once two hunters take up shooting positions, it's only a matter of time before they have to move. You're going to fire X number of shots, then the dogs are gonna hole up— scared! While on the move it's important to take up stands where you can overlook as much dog territory as possible. That way you'll be able to shoot longer before moving. Some prairie dog country is extremly flat. Such terrain doesn't lend itself to walk up type hunting. When you lie down in flat country, the sparse grass vegetation is high enough that only close shots are possible. You're often too low to see dogs that are only 50 yards away. Slightly rolling country is the best for my favorite walk up hunting. Often edges of little valleys are the

The Harris Bipod, ideal for attaching to the rifle's front swivel stud, and a lightweight, super steady rest. Note sling swivel can still be attached for easy carrying.

best to peer down into, plus you can look and shoot into hills on the opposite side.

You don't find the best "dog" shooting around areas where prairie grass is lush, though these grasses are the little rodent's main food supply. The sparser the grass, the less food supply there seems to be, the more prairie dogs there are. The reason behind this is probably that a big population of prairie dogs simply has eaten off all the succulent stuff, but I'm not so certain this is true. Be sure to keep on the lookout for minimal grass areas when scouting for potential territory.

You might consider toting some type of pack, mainly to carry an ample supply of shells when walking across a prairie dog town. Black powder supply stores and mail order outfits often have smallish leather shoulder bags that'll easily hold four or five boxes of ammo (assuming twenty rounds per box). A canteen of water is a good bet because it's often bone dry and there's a hot overhead sun on most prairie dog shoots. If you don't have a canteen on your belt, you should definitely have an ample supply of water back at the hunting vehicle. Don't permit your body to get dehydrated. That's the quickest way to get sick and ruin a potentially memorable trip. A straw cowboy hat is another essential part of any prairie dog hunt, walk-up or hunt-from-the-vehicle. Such a hat will protect its wearer from heat stroke and heat prostration. It'll also shade the eyes from bright sun when peering through the scope sight.

Be particularly aware of where you sit and lie after you have selected your shooting position. In most good prairie dog areas it'll be dry, and small prickly pear and other cactus plants can be fairly abundant. Check the ground carefully before sitting or lying down. Don't sit or lie in a patch replete with thorns or you're going to waste a lot of time picking those spines out of your skin. I recall Bob Bell sitting down to glass in one patch of prickly pear. Took him forever to get all the spines picked out of his backside. He made some picture—out there on the prairie with his pants down, picking away!

I've used a 6X scope on a prairie dog hunt and found it wasn't powerful enough. This scope was on an Ithaca LSA-55, a light bolt rifle in 308 Winchester caliber. I fired the 308's a few times, but had a good supply of 308 Accelerators from Remington on that trip. This was an excellent cartridge for dogs, zipping 55 grain soft points out at over 3700 fps, but the 6X scope wasn't up to seeing dogs at two hundred yards and beyond very clearly.

I've also used 16X and 20X scopes on the prairie. The 16X was on a Savage 112V in 25-06. The recoil from this gun is too much for more than maybe thirty shots each day, and the 16X Leupold magnified those hot day prairie heat waves too much. Distortion was naturally even more magnified in the 20X, a Lyman LBR on a Savage 112V in 220 Swift. The ideal scope is one somewhere between 6X and 16X. On a super hot day the 8X would be my choice. If no heat waves are coming off the prairie, I'd select the 12X. The 10X is the perfect compromise. Heat wave problems will be there, but they can be dealt with. Definition out to three hundred yards and more is excellent in a 10X scope with good quality glass, assuming the user has 20/20 vision, corrected or uncorrected. Those with poorer corrected vision might find 12X scopes more beneficial.

I'm particularly fond of the Weaver K Model scopes. They once came in 8X, 10X and 12X. My 12X has their Range-Finder reticle installed, but it was recently discontinued. This one has two horizontal wires that are six minutes of an angle apart. Check out each individual Range-Finder with a yardstick positioned vertically at a known one hundred yard distance to determine exactly how far the two crosswires are apart. The great benefit of two horizontal wires is that they give a more precise reference point for holdovers at distant ranges. This reticle isn't a benefit in normal 200 to 250 yard prairie dog hunting, but in shooting small varmints at more distant ranges. I'm very accustomed to the Range-Finder reticle, and I like it. These Weavers are also reasonably light, much lighter than external adjustment scopes that adorn many varmint rifles. When talking about a rifle for walking up varmints, weight is an important consideration.

Many hunters have something like a 3X-9X variable scope on their big game rifle. They may want to take that scope off the big game rig and put it on their prairie dog ordnance for the summer. I see nothing wrong with this. Wound up to 9X a variable comes close to being ideal power for most of the dog hunting anyone will encounter. Remember my guidelines—6X is not quite enough—16X is too much power.

One of the most effective ways to hunt the prairie is from a vehicle. Most states that abound with prairie dogs have no regulation against shooting from a vehicle, but it always pays to check local laws first. Some type of four wheel drive rig is best for taking off across the prairie, but even these might bog down. Generally the prairie is extremely dry. When it rains, you can bet the previously hard ground will turn to the slickest mud this side of snot. Keep an ear to the weather forecast and an eye toward the clouds. If a thunderstorm threatens, hightail it for a hard road.

In dry weather a two wheel drive vehicle has all the traction you'll ever need. Something like a pickup truck with higher road clearance is of definite benefit, but even a car can be used if the driver is particularly careful of where he drives. Still, I wouldn't suggest or recommend a car for this type of hunting. A pickup two wheel drive would be minimum for me, a four wheel drive preferable.

On private land you'll need permission to hunt, doubly so if you want to drive across a rancher's prairie. On some public hunting areas it's still possible to drive across the prairie. The only time this will be feasible is when it's dry, so there's no danger of causing any irreparable damage to the ground you drive across. Indian reservations provide some outstanding prairie dog hunting. Permission is essential.

Whenever I find a dog town in extremely flat prairie, I hunt right from the vehicle instead of on foot. Shooting takes place from the hood of the car or the roof. In either case sand bag rests are utilized. From the higher roof position, it's possible to shoot varmints from even longer range when the terrain is perfectly flat, or almost so.

The idea is to drive to the edge of a dog town and stop. If using a car or station wagon, the shooting can take place from the hood or the roof. If utilizing a pickup, the shooting can take place from the hood or a shooter can get into the bed of the truck and use the roof for a rest. A seat of the right height in the pickup bed will be most useful. In either case, only the shooter should be sitting in or leaning against the vehicle. The partner or partners, once the shooter is prepared to fire, must stand away. Otherwise their slight movements, even their breathing, can cause the shot to go off target.

While glassing for prairie dogs, however, as in woodchuck hunting, it's a good idea to balance the elbows on the vehicle while glassing

Bob Bell uses a rest on pickup roof, shooting a Savage 112V in 25-06. Some western states permit shooting from the vehicle at prairie dogs.

with binoculars, or to glass from a sandbag placed on the hood or roof. This makes for considerably more stability which results in less eye fatigue over a long day of using binoculars, and permits the glasser to observe minute detail. Thus the prairie dogs are easier to spot.

As in walking up dogs, vehicle hunters might fire their rifles two, a dozen, maybe even fifty times. Sooner or later, the within-range critters are going to head for the safety of their subterranean homes. Start the vehicle and drive a short distance. How far you move each time will be dependent on how much country you'll next be looking over and the amount of dogs using the area you can be glassing. Often the move will involve less than one hundred yards, though in other instances it'll pay to move even a mile. You should be able to stow rifles, binoculars, sandbags, etc., quickly, and be able to get them back out quickly.

Generally speaking, it will be possible to take longer shots when hunting from a vehicle compared to foot hunting. This is because the position of the rifle, off the ground and on the hood or roof of the vehicle, will be considerably higher. You'll be able to see and shoot farther from the higher position. There may be some long range purists who will prefer to shoot a lot less and concentrate on extremely long range targets. In some instances you can overlook vistas where 300, 400 and 500 yard shots will be possible. If you prefer this type of shooting, I suggest an extremely heavy rifle, say in the fifteen pound range. Such a varmint piece will aid in sucking up some of the recoil. Still, you might want to confine your shooting to one hundred rounds or less per day.

No matter how you hunt prairie dogs, it pays to wear some type of ear protection. Muffs are out of the question. It's too hot. The custom molded protectors are excellent. The least any serious prairie dog shooter should opt for are the soft foam protectors. These are light in weight and do tone down rifle muzzle blast to a significant degree. You'll never know you have them in.

The prairie dog is a member of the squirrel family. The blacktail, the one found on the prairies, is called *Cynomys ludovicianus* by the Latin minded, while the white-tailed prairie dogs of the mountain valleys is scientifically dubbed *Cynomys gunnisoni*. The dog of the high ground is generally a tad smaller, though the black-tailed is far from a big guy. He in no way comes close to the size of a woodchuck.

A mature prairie dog will measure about twelve inches in total body length, plus another three inches for his tail. A two pounder will be

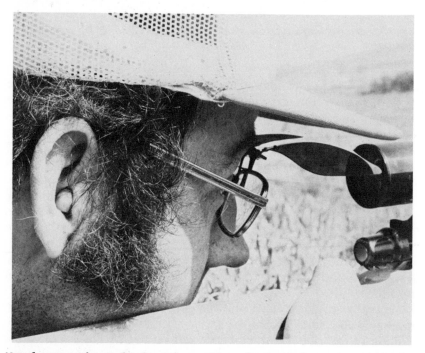

Note foam ear plug in this shooter's ear. Due to the tremendous volume of shooting on a prairie dog hunt, such hearing protectors are suggested.

typical, though three pounders are common. Their color is a tawny light brown. They have short but stout legs, which helps in excavating their underground homes. The ears are rounded.

Their holes go down at a steep angle, some of them quite deep under the prairie surface. Earth is heaped around each den opening to prevent rain run-off water from entering their dwelling place, though rain is not common during the summer season. Most of the prairie country where these little targets exist is desert-like.

These burrows are not only the prairie dog's homes, they're also his refuge. He's harassed by all manner of predators. Hawks and owls are particularly feared because they're so effective in picking unsuspecting dogs off as they're feeding above ground. Eagles even take a few, but carnivores like foxes and a few others also take their share. Nevertheless, the prairie dog's most dreaded foe is the black-footed ferret, although this species is almost extinct.

The near demise of the black-footed ferret came about because of the war the bureaucrats waged on prairie dogs. When the vast number of prairie dogs plummeted in the course of decades of intense poisoning, the black-footed ferret lost its food supply, the only source this tiny but sharp-toothed predator ever utilized. The ferrets lived in the dog towns. When they grew hungry, it was easy pickin's to enter a hole at night and make his choice—Ma, Pa or one of the little guys or gals! This ferret didn't know how to hunt anything else. There are still a smattering of black-footed ferrets around the big dog towns, but the range of these dog towns was vastly reduced by poisoning during the 50's and 60's, and even before. The outlook doesn't look bright for the black-footed ferret at this time, especially since a minor bureaucratic war against prairie dogs is still raging.

If prairie dogs ever do become extinct, the maudlin media will blame hunters, though they say nothing about the poisoning that has gone on for decades, eradicating probably billions of prairie dogs, virtually eliminating them from over two-thirds of their former haunts. The black-footed ferret has been eliminated right along with the prairie dog. But that's today's version of progress.

There's no way riflemen can have any affect on the total number of prairie dogs. Even their current habitat is too limitless, their reproductive capacity too great, and riflemen who seek them are too few and far between. Mating takes place in the early spring, and the gestation period lasts for about one month. From three to eight are born in each litter. The young stay in the burrow, nursing, for approximately seven weeks.

As mentioned previously, the dog's food supply is mainly the sparse prairie grasses, though they also eat some weeds, roots and seeds. I also mentioned that these animals tend to live where prairie grasses are extremely sparse. You might observe lusher grass areas from time to time, but the prairie dogs will seldom use them, especially large numbers of prairie dogs. I haven't figured out why they prefer the sparsest stretches of prairie grass, though perhaps some scientists have.

The prairie dog is not nocturnal. At night he stays inside the safety of his burrow, probably dreaming or fearing the next black-footed ferret intrusion, for that predator only stalks at night. When above ground the prairie dog sits on his haunches when he spots any type of danger. Immediately before diving for the safety of his den he'll often twitch his tail, head and/or body a bit, at the same time giving a vocal warning whistle. This alerts his brethren that he has spotted something awry and they'd better watch out. Shortly after this display, the dog'll dive for safety.

Prairie dog towns have a somewhat regimented form of society. A coterie is a group of prairie dogs that live together in peace. They have boundries of land they claim to be theirs, and it often butts right up against that of neighboring coteries. Within the coterie there's much show of friendship, grooming one another, plenty of mouth to mouth contact, etc. However, these niceties are never shown at the borders of what they call home, when a member of another coterie is met face to face. On these occasions there's much teeth chattering, tail spreading and anal sniffing. These acts establish territorial boundries. Neighboring coteries are thus able to live next to one another without full fledged war going on continually.

There's little question that the prairie dog is a most interesting little animal. Hopefully we'll learn even more about them in the future. There's also little question that here is one of the best targets any rifleman can choose. Any shooter who concentrates a week on prairie dog sport each spring, summer or early fall is going to be quickly awarded his Doctor of Rifle Degree. There's no other long range target on the face of the earth that is so abundant, one with whom the rifleman can pack so much intense and beneficial shooting into such a short amount of time. If you haven't hunted prairie dogs, you should— before the bureaucrats have them all poisoned off!

CHAPTER 11

Duping a Fox

Only a whisper of breeze disturbed the night air. Overhead bright winter stars sparkled with added brilliance in the frigid temperature of late January. The cassette tape in the recorder, which was turned up to full volume, was spewing forth the frantic screams of a gray fox pup in distress.

Though we had been keen and alert each time we had selected a calling spot and turned on the recorder earlier in the evening, it was now past 10 o'clock. After a lack of success at seven previous locations, the edge had worn off. I was a bit inattentive and pessimistic about our chances. Then there was a distinct sound in the pile of slash forty-five or fifty yards off to our left. I touched my partner, Jim Smith, on the coat sleeve. He had heard it too, for the dull glow of his head light was now flashing in the direction of the sound.

I was aware of my heart pounding. My right thumb fingered the safety of my 5mm rimfire rifle while my left hand reached out past the stock fore-end and found the switch of the light that was taped to the end of the rifle barrel. The cold was forgotten.

Uneventful seconds ticked past—each one painfully slow. It's always that way when game is about to show itself—but hasn't. Jim turned the volume on the tape recorder down and we waited—and waited. Less than a minute or two passed by, but that interval seemed more like half a lifetime.

Finally Jim touched my sleeve and I knew that he saw the eyes of the fox reflected in the dim light on his head. I switched on the two

cell flashlight on the rifle, peered through the scope, and there they were—two bright amber colored eyes—the first fox I had ever seen at night while calling these critters. I could barely make out the cross-hairs in my scope. The fox was moving, ever so slowly, one cautious step at a time, but moving. The form of his body was difficult to see in the limited light, but there was enough to be certain. It was a fox—probably a gray.

Finally he stopped, the safe was off now, my finger was tightening on the trigger. The crosshairs were bobbing around, but then they settled. Just before the final few ounces sent the bullet on its way, the critter moved again and I had to let up on the trigger. When he stopped the second time I noted a close, out-of-focus object in the left side of the scope. Raising my head off the stock, I confirmed my suspicions—a tree. I took one quick step to the right to have a clear field of view, but by then the quarry had vanished. We kept calling for five minutes more, but my chance to finally score on a fox we had called had vanished.

Talk about frustration! I had heard and read tales about how easy foxes, especially grays, could be duped by electronic calling. Even mouth blown predator calls that imitate the sound of a dying or dis-tressed cottontail rabbit made putting fox fur on the stretcher seem easy. Many early mornings and dusky evenings found me in good fox country, blowing a predator call or playing a rabbit squeal record. My score in all those sessions was zilch—exactly zilch! Never once had I called a critter in.

All of the calling I tried had been alone. I had never sought the advice of an expert. Finally, partly out of desperation, and partly because I simply wanted to figure out how to dupe a fox, one of our most wary varmints, I contacted a fellow in my home state who markets different types of cassette tapes, records and calls for bringing various critters within close range—Jim Smith of Summerville, PA.

Jim's an ardent outdoorsman who spends all his spare time hunting, fishing and trapping. Back in 1949, while trapping in late summer for bounty rather than pelt, Jim caught a young gray fox in one of his dirt hole sets. As he walked his trap line that particular morning he heard a fox barking and squealing in his trap. Upon approaching the trap Jim noticed another mature fox about thirty yards back in the brush, observing the trapped pup's predicament. Once the observant critter saw Jim, it melted from view.

Rather than kill the young fox in the trap, Jim decided to bring him back alive. When he picked the young gray up by the scruff of the neck to release him from the trap, the frightened gray ball of fur screamed bloody murder! Jim looked up in time to see a fox, probably the same one he noted upon approaching his trap, returning to see what all the commotion was about. That's when the gong of an idea sounded in Jim's brain—mature foxes could be called—and called in close—to the distress cries made by this young fox pup!

Jim refers to that first fox pup as a "real cry baby." He didn't have to be hurt—just picked up by the scruff of the neck and he would start screaming and barking frantically. Over the years Jim managed to trap plenty of young foxes in late summer, but only a small percentage of them ever made a sound—no matter how hard he tried to get them to squeal.

In the 50's other experts in the predator calling field experimented with rabbit distress cries and distress sounds from other animals, even birds, and found that it was possible to call in foxes, coyotes, bobcats, and many other predator type animals. While that was going on Jim Smith was having a grand time—getting afield every chance he could, holding a "cry baby" fox pup by the scruff of the neck with one hand and firing his 16 guage pump with the other hand—at grays that came to the yammering.

They came in on the run, usually—no pussyfooting around, especially in late summer. The majority of the foxes that would come in to this fox pup bark were not only grays, but females as well. Jim reasons that the mother of a litter of pups feels that one of her offspring is in danger when she hears the frantic pup squeals—and she charges in to the rescue.

It was in the early 60's when predator calling via the use of record playing machines and mouth blown calls suddenly became extremely popular, and then Jim decided to have a few records of his fox pup barks made. They sold like hot cakes, and have been selling well ever since. In the interim, Jim has added cottontail distress squeals, instruction records, predator and turkey calls, and now recently cassette tapes to his line.

The first time Jim and I got together was early in the fall. Fox bounties had been removed many years before and Jim felt the gray fox pelts (he calls in grays 75 or 80 percent of the time as reds aren't nearly as susceptible) would not yet be prime. He suggested that I arm myself with a camera instead of a rifle or shotgun.

The first several areas we tried were unproductive. Then we tried a spot where Jim had never called before. We were on the upper side of one hollow. A deep slashing where Jim hoped a fox would be resting, covered the bottom. A wide field of uncropped hay between our calling spot and the slashing would make it easy to see any fox that might answer the call.

Jim's a firm believer in drab colored or camouflage clothing, but even more importantly, he makes certain he is well hidden before he turns on his cassette tape or record player. Foxes are wary. They have sharp eyesight, and the hunter (with gun or camera) is situated right where the squeals are emanating—and that's where the incoming fox focuses his attention. It was late afternoon, and though foxes are much more active after dark, we had high hopes that this would be our first productive spot.

The call was only on about two minutes when the fox came out of the heavy cover at a semi-fast lope and ambled up along a woods edge, narrowing the distance in short order. He slowed a couple of times, but he kept coming, seemingly determined to find out exactly where the critter in distress was located.

At about twenty yards the fox stopped. Had I been carrying either a shotgun or a rifle, it would have been an easy matter to take him. Instead I was focusing, clicking, and advancing the shutter of my camera.

While I tried to remain as motionless as possible, Jim turned the volume way down and that caught the fox's curiosity even more. He advanced closer. My 200mm telephoto lens focuses to eight feet. He was almost that close before he turned and left. He didn't run off scared, he simply walked away.

I figured the action was over, but not Jim. He changed records, this time putting on a rabbit squeal imitation, and believe it or not, the fox came back. Not quite as close, but he came back. This time he returned within fifteen yards of the record machine. Again he vanished, but Jim put the fox pup distress record back on and though I find it hard to believe even now, the fox came back yet a third time, and he came back in close! Surely he smelled us, surely he must have seen us, but he seemed to lose his fear of man. He was totally concerned with the screaming fox pup. Finally I had seen a fox called up electronically—and I had the pictures to prove it, even if I didn't have a pelt yet.

We tried several more unproductive locations late that afternoon, and just as full light was waning, Jim suggested we try one final spot. I swear the record machine hadn't played ten seconds when we heard the fox coming. This one wasn't walking, he wasn't even at an easy lope. He was making a mad dash for the noise emanating from the record. But this fox wasn't as curious. He circled us quickly, got our scent, and vanished. He never stopped in the open long enough for a picture. The first short afternoon with Jim Smith convinced me that there was plenty to learn about calling these critters, and I vowed to get back and spend more time with him.

But upland bird season started the next day, and since chasing fast fliers like grouse, quail, woodcock, and other members of their feathered ilk is my favorite pastime, it was mid winter before I returned to another fox calling session.

Jim liked one particular area—an old coal stripping. We had called there during our first outing, but hadn't enjoyed any luck. The electronic call had been running about two minutes when I noted a fox high on a spoil bank to our right. On that occasion I was armed with a double barreled 12 gauge side by side, and though the fox stopped several times along the top side of that bank, offering me a shot if I had been carrying a rifle, it was too far for a shotgun—sixty yards or more.

But that fox wanted to answer the call so badly he came down over the vertical bank of that old strip. I actually saw him fall the last few yards, then he disappeared out of sight at the bottom. I fingered the safe, anticipating he would come up on our side of the stripping and within view any second. But he never showed.

Night fell shortly after that. It was a cold, cold January, and after supper I got my first taste of hunting well after dark—which Jim claims is the best time. Gray fox are nocturnal creatures. During the daytime they usually seek underground dens, and no matter how close the hunter is with the call, foxes can't hear the pleadings.

Jim also keeps a constant eye on the wind, and claims it is a waste of time to call in even a mild breeze. A still night or one with only a whisper of wind is perfect for this predator calling pastime.

On the next calm night we were back at that favorite coal stripping of Jim's, hoping to entice the same fox we had lured in before. He responded, but it took almost five minutes before he appeared—at the top of the same spoil bank where we had first seen him during the previous calling session. This time the fox found a safer place to come down over the bank—he made it to the bottom without falling! Again he disappeared from view in the hollow between us—again I found the safe, this time confident I was about to sack my first fox that responded to a call. I was carrying the 5mm rimfire with 4X scope.

Instead of coming straight up over the bank and into close view, the critter appeared about fifty yards to our left. I caught a glimpse of him out of the corner of my eye. It was evident he was circling. A lot of brush intervened, but he stopped and I began to squeeze off regardless of the intervening branches. I had spent too many hours trying to entice a fox to lose out on this chance. But he melted from view before I was able to pull the final ounces on the trigger. He was trying to get to our downwind side.

The call kept running. Long minutes elapsed. They weren't the agonizing seconds outdoorsmen go through when they feel that game is about to appear any moment. Instead they were doubtful moments, for I judged that fox had winded us and he would never be seen again.

Jim guessed the gray was making a 360 degree circle and he might appear on top of the spoil bank where we had seen him originally. Jim was looking at the top of that bank, hoping to get a shot with his .222 while I was scanning the area where I had last seen the fox in my scope.

The Burnham Brothers BB-CC-1 cassette caller on foxes. The gunner is well camouflaged. Note speaker in background.

Out of the corner of my eye I glimpsed something to the left. I jerked my head around in time to see the face of a fox looking directly at me. There was no time for a shot. Upon seeing me the fox immediately turned tail and disappeared. As he turned he kicked up enough rocks that Jim heard the commotion. My partner whirled in time to see the fox dart behind a pine. How the fox had gotten so close is a mystery. He had silently covered fifteen yards of open strip mine shale, not a blade of cover, before I discovered his presence.

My next session with Jim provided the excitement described in the opening paragraphs of this story. I still didn't have a pelt to sell to the fur buyer. Four times I had enjoyed calling sessions with Jim Smith, and on each of those occasions Jim had shown me one or more foxes. That proves that experts who know what they are doing can successfully call them in—and call them in close. But putting a fox pelt on the fur stretcher is something else.

The whole point of the foregoing is that foxes aren't easy varmints to bag, whether you're using the latest in electronics or the finest, most pleading mouth call made. The nature of a fox is to be extremely wary. They can, of course, be called in. After many frustrations afield, the law of averages catches up with the fox. When this happens, it's sometimes amazing how foolish they can seem.

Through the telling of the foregoing personal experiences, it'll be easy for the reader to pick out tips that'll help him score on the challenging gray. If you want a red fox in your sights, better be prepared to invest in a four wheel drive vehicle, in case you don't already have one, and spend a lot of money on gasoline cruising back roads in winter. Sunny days are best. That's often when reds love lying out in the snow, often in an open field—at least a resonably open field. In this condition you might attempt a close shot with a shotgun, though most will have a flat shooting varmint rifle in the vehicle. A long range shot can be tried shortly after sighting the sunning red.

Yet another way to hunt foxes is with the aid of a pack of hounds. My buddy Paul Hollobaugh and I used to do that plenty. There's excitement galore on these hunts. Once the dogs have the quarry up and running ahead, the degree of excitement shifts into high gear. Some prefer to follow the dogs as the chase progresses, and I'm one of them. Often a good fox chase, especially one involving a red, progresses for one heck of a long distance. Consequently, sticking with the hounds involves lots of physical endurance. Other fox hound hunters take up stands at strategic locations, often at crossings foxes have used previously. Some opt for rifles for this type of hunting, but the majority carry shotguns. No matter which you're carrying, there's a fair bet you'll have a good chance for a shot—if you were carrying the other. Shotgun toters always have rifle opportunities, and vice versa.

Lately, fox calling is far more popular than chasing them with hounds or driving winter roads and trying to spot reds from afar with binoculars as they sun on the snow. In some states electronic calls are prohibited, and in others the regulations governing their use sometimes changes. I won't attempt to zero in on each state's regulations, for some of them would change between writing and publication. Electronic calls aren't more effective than mouth blown calls. It's simply that mouth blown calls are more difficult to master. They take effort, experience and savvy. All that is provided on a cassette, 8-track tape or record. Consequently electronic calls make it easier for more people to enjoy predator calling.

While bobcats and coyotes also come to electronic and mouth blown calls, no effort is being made in this book to offer how-to information on these species. Due to extremely high pelt value, plenty of both are being harvested. In some states non-residents are not permitted to hunt one or the other, plus there is at least some pressure in some areas to eliminate hunting one or the other, at least for the immediate future.

146

CHAPTER 12

Crows

I've killed crows with varmint rifles, and so have numerous other varmint hunters. We'll all kill more in the future, too. Still, for most every outdoorsman who puts any time into crow hunting, this is a shotgun rather than a rifle game. There are a couple of reasons why this will always be true. Crows have to be on the ground before it becomes safe to shoot at them with a rifle. If they're in trees it means the shooter doesn't know where his bullet is going to come to rest. When on the ground, crows tend to be super wary. By the time an approaching rifleman spots them and gets his varmint rifle situated on his rest, the black marauder has spooked and is flapping his wings toward safer sites.

Couple these traits with the simple fact that a crow is a bird, a critter that flies. Flying birds are what shotgunning is all about. The crow is also responsive to calling, like a turkey, a goose or a mallard, and responsive to decoys. With all the foregoing in mind, there's little wonder why the crow offers so much more for shotgunners than for riflemen.

The common crow's Latin name is *Corvus brachyrhynchos*. No reader needs a description of a crow. You all know what they look like. The only bird with much similarity is the raven, though it is much larger. Crows typically measure from seventeen to twenty-one inches from tip of beak to tip of tail. They are indigenous to most of the country, with the possible exception of the far west. They tend to breed and summer in northern regions (well into Canada, too) and winter in more southerly portions.

Setting out the crow decoys and an owl decoy prior to a crow calling session.

As with a lot of other varmint hunting, there's seldom much competition on a crow shoot. It's a wonder that legions of shotgunners aren't addicted to crow calling and out every weekend, but they're not. I have **NEVER** been afield and encountered another crow hunter. I can't make that statement about any other type of hunting.

The crow has a great deal going for it. Wonderfully adaptable, it can subsist on a wide variety of both vegetable and animal matter. As agricultural and/or forest conditions change, the crow is able to arrange his diet and life schedule to coincide with them. He'll live within close proximity to man, yet he'll almost never permit himself to be pot shot by the average hunter. His natural wariness helps him get away in the nick of time again and again.

Assuming you haven't hunted crows much, if at all, how can you go about enjoying some success with this challenging shotgun target? First you have to convince yourself that crows can see much better than you can, and that you're going to have to go overboard with camouflage. You need a complete camo outfit, pants, jacket, hat, but don't stop there. You'll also need a face mask, or face make up (normally this stick makeup is marketed to turkey or bow and arrow deer hunters) and camo gloves. Even when so somberly attired, you'll still have to get completely hidden, so well out of sight that you'll hardly be able to shoot. Only by convincing yourself that all this tomfoolerly is necessary, then doing it, can you expect to bring these wary black birds within shotgun range with any degree of consistency.

The next necessity requires a significant outlay of cash—for an electronic call. The one I'm currently using is the Burnham Brothers (Marble Falls, TX 78654) Model BB-CC-1 Cassette Caller. It consists of a cassette recorder, amplifier, battery chamber and speaker. The amplifier and speaker are necessary, for they greatly increase volume, permitting you to reach far out from your selected stand and bring in crows from a long way off. This rig, with a supply of cassette tapes, will set you back less than a brace of C-notes.

I've doctored my BB-CC-1 caller a bit. The cassette recorder had some shine to it, though it was mostly dull black. I went over the shiny places with a black Magic Marker. Now sun won't glint from it into a crow's eyes. While the bottom of this caller is a dull green plastic, the top is a light buff color. I bought a can of flat black spray paint and toned down the color of the top of this box. The flat black spray paint can also be used to go over crow decoys occasionally.

With an electronic crow call a totally camouflaged hunter who carefully chooses each of his calling spots is going to have consistent success. Don't assume from that statement that electronic crow calls make it easy to kill these black marauders in wholesale numbers, for they won't. They will permit the hunter to call in some birds at most every calling spot. He may or may not kill one or two of them; then

The Burnham Brothers BB-CC-1 cassette caller. The hunter is all rigged in camo gear, including face mask.

again, he may not kill any. Kill success of this magnitude isn't going to harm the crow population one bit.

Only by learning a great deal more about crow habits and how to be a more effective hunter will anyone graduate from tyro to expert status. You can easily go out and enjoy one slight success after another with crows, simply by using that electronic squawk box and by staying completely hidden in camo from head to toe.

Electronic calls may not be legal for crows in every state. If there are any which legislate against its use, they're few and far between. Check with authorities to be certain, before you make your investment. Electronic calls are not permitted for ducks, geese, turkeys, and in some states for predators like foxes, but hunting crows with an electronic call is permitted by most.

Learning to call crows effectively with a mouth call isn't easy. Back in the 30's, 40's, 50's, even the early 60's, there were a fair number of crow calling experts. They understood and could speak crow language better than your high school Spanish prof could enunciate "muy bueno." These experts could and did pass their knowledge to youngsters who were interested enough to ask and willing to work hard at both study and practice calling. But shortly after the early 1960's crow hunting changed. Crow numbers went way down. Most biologists blamed DDT, but I doubt anyone knows for sure why their numbers waned. It makes sense to blame DDT. Like the many hawks whose populations also plummeted, crows are at the end of the food chain and thus tend to absorb great amounts of this long lived poison.

When the yearning to hunt crows with a passion fizzled because there were fewer and fewer crows to hunt, so did the knowledge of how to entice these birds effectively with mouth blown calls. A similar circumstance happened when the season on snipe was closed from the late 1930's to the early 1950's. During that period an entire generation of snipe hunters died out. These sportsmen had learned the snipe hunting trade from their fathers and uncles. With no snipe to hunt, experts couldn't pass on their knowledge to youngsters. As a consequence, few if any of today's sportsmen know much at all about hunting, calling and decoying snipe effectively. Though today's seasons are long, bag limits extremely liberal, and the snipe is a gourmet's delight on the table, current estimates indicate this long bill is the most underharvested of all game birds, with hunters taking less than two percent of the annual population. Every year there's a sixty to eighty percent snipe loss due to natural mortality, so, as far as human consumption is concerned, 58 to 78 percent of the nation's snipe literally goes to waste every season. The comparison would be to harvesting two percent of an annual corn crop!

I believe that the only reason we have any crow hunters at all today is due to the electronic call. It would be impossible for a tyro to go out with a mouth blown call and experience anything but very occasional success.

Okay! Camo gear, an electronic call and being well hidden are the three factors that contribute to quick success at tyro crow hunting. What are some other tips and suggestions that will help the hunter be more effective?

Buy a mouth blown call. Use it sparingly at first, in conjunction with the tape on your electronic call. Avoid three quick "caws." This is the crow's alarm signal. After turning on your squawk box, start giving one occasional mouth caw, or maybe a two caw sequence. I've found that if crows are reluctant to come into the electronic call, and you're certain they're within hearing range, some mouth blown calls, in conjunction with the tape sounds, can mean the difference.

I've also found that it pays to use the mouth blown call if you've called crows in, they've circled high without coming down close enough for a shot, then they start to leave. A couple of mouth blown caws under this condition usually brings them right back.

Once you know birds are on their way, stop blowing the mouth call. Let your electronic marvel take over for you. After you shoot and the birds start to leave, start blowing again. You don't need much from a mouth blown call that you're blowing to augment whatever is em-

anating from the tape, but I'm certain mouth calling helps in several specific circumstances.

If you and a buddy or two are hunting together, have everyone blow their call, at least a little, especially if it's under the right circumstances. Each of you also should have different sounding calls. In the wild most every crow sounds slightly different, so three different callers should all sound a bit different. If you hunt alone most of the time you should have at least two crow calls around your neck, maybe even three. Not only will you be able to sound like different crows each time you put a different one into your mouth, crow calls do break down—maybe a split reed, maybe you'll even bite the stem in two during a particularly exciting period. Sometimes excess moisture puts a call out of commission for a time. A spare call or two under any of these conditions will keep you hunting.

While cassette electronic calls aren't the only type available today, they are the most popular. The first electronic calls available were record machines with amplifiers and speakers. One called the "Call of the Wild" was the rage. Now the choice is mainly cassette or 8-track tape callers with amplifier and speaker. All these units are battery operated, either C and/or D cells or the bigger, rectangular 6 volt batteries (usually two required).

In the future, with micro electronics coming on strong, I'm predicting much smaller units than those now available. Once microcircuitry gets into electronic game calls, weight and bulk are going to be vastly reduced. I can envision the day when a top quality crow call will involve little more than a space for a smallish battery or batteries, a place to install a cassette tape, the speaker and the wire. All the required circuitry will fit into a space no bigger than one's thumb nail. The advantage to the crow hunter will be significant. Currently I have trouble carrying crow decoys. My hands are full—with shotgun, squawk box containing the batteries, amplifier and speaker, and the cassette recorder. If I can free one hand so I can tote a burlap sack full of crow decoys, maybe one paper-mâché owl, I'll probably increase my average calling success at each blind site.

Back to more calling tips. Once you have crows coming to the call, you should not only cease mouth blowing, you should also ease back on the volume of the squawker. I like to start off at max volume unless I can hear crows a relatively short distance away. If you have crows circling your blind out of gun range, slowly ease back on the volume. This often makes them curious enough to fly lower, often low enough for a shot.

Because you have to be able to adjust volume from time to time, you must be positioned **at** the cassette recorder. Usually speakers which plug into the amplifier have cords measuring about fifteen feet. When possible, position the speaker that full cord length away from you. The advantage of this tip is that it moves the noise of the caller as far away from you as possible, thus you're able to hear incomers and overhead crows more easily. With the squawk box close to your ear it's very difficult to hear live, incoming crows. Hearing those incomers and overhead birds is a major advantage. You're better prepared to swing that shotgun into action if you know a shot is probable at any second. When crows take you by surprise, you might not get a shot off.

What about blind selection? Experience will help. Some locations are perfect blind sites. Others are lousy. Most fall somewhere in between. Learning to determine top potential calling spots is a key to consistent success. Whenever possible, lean toward stands on higher ground, little crests, ridges, etc. Bottoms of hollows tend to be poor choices. When crows come to your calling they'll naturally tend to follow contours. Higher ground puts you closer to them, lower grounds put you farther away. With a shotgun in your hands, distance is always of prime consideration.

When the leaves are off the trees (fall, winter and early spring), I like to look for pine stands, especially low ones. Pines provide dense overhead foliage, no matter the season. Consequently a camouflaged hunter who doesn't budge in a dense pine stand is going to be almost impossible to pick out, even for a wary-eyed crow. Low pines are better than maturing pines because crows circling overhead will tend to be within closer range more often.

Without pines I look for dense vegetation, the lower and denser, the better. You can never be too well hidden from a darn crow. Don't select a stand so you have a broad expanse of open sky above, thinking that you'll need that open sky to shoot through. At the perfectly selected crow stand there should be very little open sky above, perhaps only a relatively small opening or two. Remember, if you have lots of sky above you, you're making it too easy for the overhead crows to spot you, even if you are adorned in camo from stem to stern. Furthermore, crows answering the call are going to circle overhead repeatedly. Eventually a bird will glide over one of the little patches of open sky above you.

In the summer leaf foliage is so dense there are often no openings to shoot through. This is when you might have to select blind sites along fence rows, or in low vegetation which hides you when in the kneeling position. When you stand up to shoot, there's no vegetation above. Realize that blind sites in summer must be necessarily different from blind sites selected when the leaves are off the trees.

One late summer blind site I particularly favor is a standing corn field. It's always essential to secure permission before entering a farmer's unharvested corn field, but I don't get many refusals. Be very careful not to damage or tramp over any of his stalks. Standing corn hides the camouflaged hunter perfectly, and crows tend to fly over

154

corn at relatively low altitudes. They don't seem to be as wary when coming into a call emanating from a corn field as they do when coming into a call that comes from pines, a woodlot, or some other dense vegetation.

When crows are circling or coming in, the hunter has to be looking up. A bright shiny face is certain to spook the quarry. I've already spoken about the necessity of wearing a face mask or greasing your face with camo paint. I've used the paint, but feel it's too messy, too much of a pain to clean off. Besides, if I stop in at a Greasy Spoon for a cup of java to go, I feel uncomfortable about all the stares and sneers. Penns Woods, 19 West Pittsburgh St., Delmont, PA 15626, makes one face mask I like. It consists of mesh camo material built around a pair of lensless eyeglass frames. Another I like is a pull on headnet (also camo mesh) with eye holes. It's from Ben Rogers Lee, Coffeeville, AL 36524. I wear glasses, but I can't wear them with a face mask. With a mask on my breathing fogs my glasses. Consequently, just before I turn on my electronic caller, I don a face mask and remove my glasses. The advantage of using camo grease paint is that you have full peripheral vision. With any type of face mask you can't see quite as much to the sides.

Windy conditions are not good for crows. They can't hear you calling, and they don't like to fly. I favor early mornings until around noon. I don't see much difference in success on cloudy days compared to sunny days, but the birds can spot you easier when it's brighter. When it's sunny, make certain you hide in the shade.

When I spot a potential calling spot while driving my vehicle, I like to get out and listen for a few minutes. If I hear a crow call I can almost always entice something. They may not come within range for a shot. If I don't hear any crows in the distance after a couple of minutes of listening, I may set up anyway, especially if the blind site is near perfect.

Once I start the machine, I like to call for at least ten minutes. Many times crows will hear your squawk box immediately, but they'll be so far off they don't know what it's saying. Several minutes may go by for them to figure out what's going on. Then they'll take wing, flying toward the sound.

Even when birds are close, they may not come immediately to the call. Once I spotted a pair of crows in a tree, and a perfect blind, but it was only one hundred yards away from the roosting birds. I had to make a big circle to get in the proper blind position. Eventually I started the machine and got ready for a sure kill or two. I couldn't believe it. Five minutes of calling produced nothing. Disgusted, I shut off the machine, unloaded my 1100, looked up, and there were both crows coming to the previous calling—two wide open shots at about twenty-five yards, and there I was, kneeling with an empty auto-loader.

Again, my advice is call for ten minutes minimum, regardless of the conditions.

Many times one, two or three birds are sent in by the larger flocks—sentries. You must kill all the sentries. If they return to the flock after being shot at, you can wager your payday wallet that no member of that flock is going to come to your calling. In spring, males and females are often paired off. If you consistently call in two birds, you can assume they're husband and wife. When an entire flock comes to your calling right from the start, most or all of them will stay beyond gun range as they circle. It's tough to fool a big flock, but maybe one or two of them can be suckered in close enough by reducing the volume on the squawk box. The best shoots are the ones where you kill all the sentries, quickly set them up to augment your decoy spread; then the rest of the flock comes in madder 'n hell.

A shell pouch attached to your belt is the best way to carry your ammo. These pouches, typically used on trap and skeet fields, will easily digest a full box of 25, and getting at them when you're ready to stuff more in your gun's magazine is easy.

I like the 12 gauge for crows, because shooting them is consistently a long range proposition. I've never subscribed much to the "any gun you have will be fine" attitude for any form of shotgunning, and crows are no exception. Any bird that is shot at 40, 45, 50 yards and more takes plenty of killing. The 20 and the 16 might be OK, but the 12 is the gun that the master crow hunter will carry.

Some might opt for the modified choke, but I favor the full. I get ten shots beyond forty yards for every three I get inside that range. I also take plenty of extra long range crow shots, those beyond fifty yards. While I wouldn't think of such long range trys at game like geese, ducks, etc., I have no compunctions about long range shots at varmints like crows. Frankly, there's a great deal of satisfaction in scratching down those ebony bedecked marauders that are flying halfway up in the stratosphere.

I've killed crows with 1½, 1⅜, 1¼, 1⅛ and 1 ounce 12 gauge loads. They all work. Most times my shell pouch is full of 1⅛ ouncers, though. When a great amount of shooting is packed into a short period, and sometimes this is what crow hunting is all about, stiff loads like the 1½, 1⅜ and 1¼ ouncers recoil too much, at least for me. The 1⅛ ounce load does not destroy my shoulder, no matter how many times I pull the trigger—if I'm shooting a gas operated auto-loader.

I've also shot crows with 4's, 6's, 7½'s and 8's. Many will tell you that 7½'s are all you need, and they will do nicely. But I've bagged too many extra long range crows with 4's and 6's. The bigger pellet sizes hold their velocity better than smaller ones at the max ranges. A crow hit in the breast with a number 4 pellet can't stand it. He's coming down. Hit in the same place with a 7½, he may or may not come down. At sixty yards 7½'s don't have the pattern density to overcome their vastly reduced energy.

The gas operated auto-loader sucks up recoil significantly. I favor them for any type of hunting where I'm going to be doing a lot of shooting in a short period of time. I also like the idea of having three shots instead of two, the max a shooter has in a side by side or an over and under. In the uplands, behind good bird dogs, the third shot is almost never necessary. In crow hunting you'll fire three shots a high percentage of the time, this because of multiple targets in the air, and when trying to knock down one more sentry before he goes back to warn the rest of the flock. If you like pump guns, they also have the three shot capability.

Until a few years ago there was no closed season on crows. Because of provisions in an international treaty, the Fish and Wildlife Service was forced to close the spring nesting season. Now all states have some type of crow regulation, and many of them change from year to year. Check your local laws. In my home state crow hunting is permitted Friday, Saturday, and Sunday, from the first weekend in June until late November when deer season opens. The Game Commission then doesn't have to listen to deer poachers carrying rifles who proclaim they're crow hunting. Crows become fair game again for three day weekends in early January, on to about the second weekend in April when it closes again. This allows three days of hunting each week for about nine and a half months, certainly a liberal season.

Why kill crows in the first place? No one takes them home and drops them in a stew pot! Crows cause damage, mainly nesting damage with respect to other birds. Song birds in particular come under crow attack, but so do nests of upland species like ruffed grouse. The crows break the eggs with their beaks. Sometimes they eat what's inside, sometimes they don't. Couple these shenanigans with the fact that crows are wary, difficult to fool, susceptible to calling and decoys, and they present a challenging flying target. What more need be said?

CHAPTER 13

Pest Pigeons

The next time you see a flock of pigeons, stop what you're doing and take time to watch them carefully. What great flyers! You won't watch them long before you come to realize that the common pigeon loves to be airborne, and to perform aerial acrobatics. In my view there isn't a tougher target a shotgunner can pit himself against. If pigeons lived in entangling cover like grouse and woodcock, and would perform their aerial stunt shows in the thicket, there would only be scattered empties in the covert, and a total lack of pigeon feathers littering the leaves.

A tyro who tries a day gunning pest pigeons will be so demoralized he may have to arrange an appointment with a shrink. He'll need professional help to explain why he is so incompetent with his scattergun. Pigeons put everyone in their place—first timers, seasoned experts and every shooter in between. Every now and then we all rake down the occasional high flyer though. That's when we extract the empty from the chamber, raise the still smoking end to our lips, and blow the Red Dot vapors away, acting cocky, like there was nothing to it.

There's not a reader in the country who can't find some pigeons to hunt, nor most other countries either. Pigeons are everywhere. Talk about adaptability! They've taken to every form of man's architecture imaginable. The little eaves and ledges we incorporate into building after building fit into the pigeon's game plan for life perfectly. They use such places to make love, to rear their young, for brawls with one

159

another, for strutting their stuff, to prop their feet up and rest between all else they do. Yes, also for bathrooms. Without architecture's eaves and ledges, our pest pigeon population would never have mushroomed.

The common pigeon is also known as the rock dove; in Latin *Columbia livia.* The bird was domesticated centuries ago, then used for food, and, because of their great homing instincts, for message carrying. The pest pigeon we all know in this country is anything but domesticated. He's as wild as they come. He has a kissin' cousin out west, called the band-tailed pigeon. Bandtails are not pests that live around city buildings, but true wild birds that live their life in the forest and its edges. Several western states give them game bird status where numbers are plentiful, with open and closed seasons as well as specified bag limits. The bandtail is no varmint. The pest pigeon, on the other hand, fits every description of varmint that Noah Webster ever came up with. Very few people think highly of pest pigeons, except fellas like me who love to watch them fly, marveling at their unbelievable aerial antics. Yep, I love to watch pigeons, but I love to shoot 'em even more. If you haven't tried this sport, you're missing out on the best pure wingshooting challenge on the face of the earth.

The little town where I live had so many pigeons they hired a couple of other hunters and myself to shoot them. A fella feels a little apprehensive standing on the town bridge, the local gendarme looking over his shoulder. The local yokel tagged along so little old ladies in tennis shoes wouldn't give me any hassle. I'd pick my shots when birds were only up or down river, so my spent pellets wouldn't rain down on any of the town's buildings, or our citizens. Frankly, even though I killed plenty of Apollo's pigeons, I never harmed our pigeon population one iota. Right now there are more flying around town than ever.

The pigeon problem in our little borough is an economic one. These ruthless birds defoul everything they touch, especially abandoned buildings, certain houses, church roofs and church steeples. The roofs and steeples are the hardest hit. After about ten years of absorbing pigeon excrement, replacement is the only answer—usually a five figure answer!

Our birds leave town during the day to forage around the outlying farm fields. This is when they're a great shotgun challenge. Make no mistake about it, pigeons aren't dumb. They don't take long to learn their lessons, but they are creatures of habit, and they can be suckered in with decoys.

While hunting geese on Maryland's Eastern Shore a couple of years ago, I marveled at a batch of pigeons zooming around the nearby silo, and remarked about them to our goose guide. We had already limited out on Canadas and were telling lies over the last of the coffee.

"You hunt pigeons?" he asked.

"You bet," was my comeback.

"Ever use taxidermy decoys?" the interrogator went on.

Wrinkling my brow I replied, "No."

"Ya otta try it." My new friend then went into a dissertation about how he and a buddy hunted pigeons all over the Eastern Shore—all summer long—and decoyed them with taxidermy decoys! Ever since that conversation I've been wanting to have someone make me up thirty taxidermy pigeon decoys, but I've never had it done. Actually, I don't know anyone other than a taxidermist who could do it, and I'm afraid to ask one how much they would cost. I do know that taxidermy Canada goose decoys are absolutely lethal. I bet taxidermy pigeon decoys would be equally as effective.

The idea would be to position these natural looking decoys in fields that local pigeons have been frequenting, then find a way to hide yourself, preferably along the edge of a fencerow. I've never tried one, but a dove call sounds a bit like a pigeon. It might get their attention; then the pests will hopefully spot your decoy spread next.

But field hunting isn't the way most pigeons meet up with a dose of chilled 7½'s. If they're gonna meet their maker via lead poisoning, chances are better than ten to one it'll be around a feedlot or farm buildings they've been known to frequent. Since they defoul both feedlots and farm buildings, you shouldn't have any problem obtaining hunting permission, even though you might be shooting right from the farmer's backyard.

Many farmers mumble several unprintable words when I request pigeon shooting permission. They're not mumbling foul words about me, but about the confounded pigeons whose droppings are rotting wood and dripping down everywhere. Then the farmers turn away, still mumbling oaths. Sometimes it's as if they haven't even replied to my request to shoot a few of those critters, but I sense from their deep hate for this low life with feathers that it's okay.

The game plan is usually to chase the residing pigeons off with the first volley of shooting, then wait for the birds' return. Typically they come back in small bunches, three, five, seven. Singles are unusual.

Rich Drury, Ray Rzeszatarski and I hunt one cattle feedlot as often as possible. The birds nest and roost in a nearby industrial plant. The farmer uses expensive feed to fatten his whiteface cattle for market—in a feeder that keeps the chow coming 24 hours a day, seven days a week. This farmer hates those pigeons with a passion that borders on psychosis. The first volley of the day is for the farmer. We stuff our shotguns full of shells, then sneak up to the barn. Many birds are down in the feeder, but the bulk will be on the barn roof above. Sometimes there are a hundred birds up there, often two or three times that many. When they flush we flock shoot, emptying our guns. As I said, the first

volley is for the farmer's benefit. After that it's all challenging shooting, as the birds start flying back.

There have been days when we've each fired more than a hundred shells, a few days when we've fired a lot more than that. I remember one Sunday best. The pests kept returning and returning, one bunch taking a volley of 7½'s only to be quickly followed by another. Rich Drury had made previous arrangements to have dinner with his family at 1 o'clock that afternoon. By noon, when he should have been leaving, the shooting was just as fast and furious as it had been when we arrived at 8 o'clock that morning. Rich put off leaving for awhile, but kept repeating how he, ". . . . had to git goin'."

I enjoyed rubbing in the fact that he had to leave. "You can't leave this, Rich. This is heaven on earth. You'll wait ten years to encounter a day like this."

Finally he clutched his empty hull bag close to his bosom and dejectedly started for his pickup. He hadn't gone ten yards when Ray injected, "Here they come again!" Rich dropped his hull bag and shot right with us. After the volley he hurried back to take up his hiding position with us again. Ten minutes later he ". . . had to get goin'" again, but incomers kept him from getting all the way back to his vehicle and leaving. Finally, about 2 o'clock, he simply bit the bullet

162

and left. I chortled him the entire way back about how crazy he was for leaving the Valhalla we found. He was an hour and a half late for Sunday dinner, so it was stone cold, plus he had to endure the icy stares of the family who couldn't understand why stupid pest pigeons would take precedence over a Sunday family dinner. Some of us have warped senses of values.

You could burn a barnful of gasoline trying to find even one suitable pigeon feedlot or farm building roost. The main reason more people don't hunt pigeons is probably because it takes that travel-the-back-roads effort, and so much of it. Then, when you find pigeon heaven you can only shoot it a couple of times a year, otherwise the quarry becomes too wary and wise. Feedlots tend to produce more consistent shooting than farm buildings, farm buildings that don't have feeders directly below. Pigeons that use barns and silos for roosting before flying out to feed in surrounding fields are easiest to spook. Shooting once a year is often all they'll stand. They don't come back after the first volley if shot repeatedly. The point is, if you're going to hunt pigeons often, you have to locate many, many potential hunting sites. Be prepared to dig deep in your pocket for gas money.

Once you find the birds, asking permission comes next. In the same breath you have to both ask for the privilege to hunt and guarantee that you won't do any damage. Farmers are understandably hyper about having their expensive buildings or livestock peppered with shot. When making your approach, it pays to have shaved that morning, and that your clothes don't look like they've been scavanged from the local dump. A bath in sweet water might not be necessary, but a neat looking appearance never hurt anyone's chances of securing permission to hunt.

Pound for pound there isn't a bird with more vitality, nor one that's tougher to kill than a common pigeon. If you don't believe me, ask the guys who shoot live pigeons competitively. I normally opt for a 12 gauge auto-loader with full choke and high antimony, extra hard 7½'s. Sixes are excellent, too. Rich usually brings his Winchester Super X auto-loader with modified choke. We both have these semi barrels fitted with Jesse Briley's screw-in chokes (Briley Manufacturing, 1035 Gessner C., Houston, TX 77055). Ray normally also shoots a Super X.

I guess in most states it would be legal to remove the plug from a semi or auto-loader when hunting pest pigeons, since they're not a game bird. Rich usually has his Super X plug out. I haven't tried it often, but may start. Guess I'm always afraid I'll forget to put the plug back in when I venture off somewhere to hunt something else. When a flock wings in close, it's sometimes possible to empty five shots while they're still in range. Because of the many multiple shot possibilities when hunting pest pigeons, I prefer the pump or auto-loader. Even with the plug installed, the shooter has three shots available. That's

better than the two in a side-by-side or over-and-under. You might hear or read about fellas who can shoot a two holer, crack it open, load and get off two more shots with lightning quickness, but they're few and far between—more often fantasies than real life shotgunners.

Because of the way gas operated auto-loaders suck up recoil, I strongly favor them over pumps, side-by-sides and over-and-unders. This is especially true when a great deal of 12 gauge shooting is expected, and I always expect plenty on a pest pigeon shoot. I might not always fire the gun as many times as I'd like, but at least I expect to shoot plenty.

Pumps can be a disadvantage to any shooter who is unfamiliar with them. With semis, side-by-sides and over-and-unders, the only physical act required is pulling the trigger. Performing that one act at the precise correct time, consistently, is most difficult for most of us. With pumps not only must the trigger be operated properly, the action must be worked manually as well. Smooth pump gun operation only comes after considerable practice. No one picks one up the first year and handles one like a twenty year veteran. The violent motion of working the action quickly, unless one is extremely smooth, also jars the barrel away from the target momentarily—another disadvantage in case one misses, and we're all prone to do that occasionally. Sometimes a pump gun shooter works the action twice without knowing it. When this happens the chamber ends up empty, a live shell on the ground (called double shucking). Another possible problem is trying to work the action when one should be pulling the trigger. The stress of shooting excitement sometimes crosses up the brain. This seldom happens with a guy who has grown up shucking a Model 12 or 870, but a dude adorned in his first pair of L.L. Beans is gonna have trouble. Still, pump guns have their champions, and many expert shotgunners shoot them very well. They tend to be slightly less expensive than auto-loaders.

Side-by-sides and over-and-unders are fine, even though my usual choice is the semi for pigeons. Since I write a great deal about shotguns, I use everything in the course of any given year. We all know there's something both nostalgic and traditional about "two holers," particularly the side by each variety. If you carry one on a pigeon hunt, I'd suggest that it weigh at least eight pounds, preferably more. I have a Remington 3200 over-and-under that hefts a few ounces over nine pounds. It sucks up repetitive recoil beautifully, but a nine pound 1100 sucks up even more.

While any gauge can be used, there's no question that the 12 is the one for pigeons. Since these birds are extra tough, it pays to put as much lead in the sky as your shoulder will handle. Some shooters will be able to stand 1¼ ounce loads all day long if using a gas operated auto-loader. I can't. Sometimes I'll fire 25 1¼ ounce loads at the start of a pigeon hunt, but then I switch to the 1⅛ ouncers. It's tough to buy a new 16 gauge any more, and I wouldn't advise purchasing a used one. In time, with few if any making 16 gauge guns, ammo will be tougher and tougher to find. So will reloading components. It is possible to make up 1⅛ ounce 16 gauge loads, the same weight I recommend for the 12, or to buy them, though the latter is tougher.

Many will think the 20 gauge ideal, since it recoils less. The latter it will do with standard loads, but the 20 won't stay with a 12 in pigeon killing power—no way. Of course, under certain conditions when totally unwary pigeons are setting their wings and coming right into the feeder, only twenty yards from the muzzle, even a 410 will perform yeoman duty in the hands of an expert. Trouble is, long range shots tend to be the rule with pigeons—forty yards, fifty yards, even more if you're willing to swing far enough ahead of these zingers.

Anyone who gets serious about hunting pigeons is going to start reloading. Otherwise he'll have to dip into the cookie jar budget to buy factory fodder. The Mrs. won't think much of that. There's plenty of savings in "rolling your own" for pest pigeons. All manner of re-loading manuals describe how to concoct the right recipe of ounces of shot, with specific primer, with specific hull, with specific wad, with specific powder. Follow such recipes to the letter. The only recom-mendation I make is to purchase high antimony, extra hard 7½'s and/or 6's for pigeons. Three companies make this shot. All American calls theirs All American 6%, Lawrence calls theirs Lawrence *Magnum,* Re-mington calls theirs Remington *RXP.* This harder shot deforms less during the trauma of set back or powder ignition, and during the potentially abrasive trip down the gun barrel. Since these harder pellets stay round instead of deforming, there are fewer that fly out of the pattern. The result is denser patterns, just what the pigeon hunter is looking for when he is swinging far, far ahead of fast flying *Columbia livia* at fifty yards.

Don't forget—the next time you see a group of pigeons, pull off the road. Take time to watch them. You'll be amazed at their acrobatics. To perform as they do, pest pigeons have to be remarkable physical specimens. This characteristic is what makes them the toughest, most challenging target a shotgunner will ever swing on.

CHAPTER 14

Starlings

Starlings, those dastardly birds brought over from Europe, are the nation's most underrated, under harvested and under utilized varmint. Here's the perfect bird for an outdoorsman who wants to master the art of shotgunning. No limits, no need for compunctions no matter how many you kill. Heck, they even taste all right. I've had 'em as part of a "black bird" pie, and the breast meat goes well as an addition to spaghetti sauce.

Most shotgunners never consider starlings, and it's a wonder they don't concentrate on them during the off season. Starlings are migratory, and no bird has done so well in response to our current agricultural practices, practices that mean plenty of waste grain left in the fields, fields without fence rows. Starlings are birds that love to flock together. Due to the sheer numbers of these flocks, they can wreck havoc with a small seed crop that's almost ready to harvest, and their droppings can be so heavy and concentrated that disease results. The latter is particularly true of starling flocks that zero in on cattle and pig feed lots. So many birds come in to feed in such places, especially if the ground is snow covered and frozen so they can't feed where they normally do, that pigs and cattle become ill with various diseases, mostly virus oriented. Even numerous humans have been known to come down with a serious virus that is carried and transmitted by huge starling flocks. Attempts to mass murder these horrendous marauders almost always fail.

Starlings aren't easy to hunt, especially those huge flocks. There are too many pairs of eyes looking for possible danger. I remember spend-

ing one full day in northwestern Tennessee trying to get just one shot at several mammoth bunches that were feeding on the ground on waste grain, with thousands of others resting in nearby trees (perhaps sentries). I never dented a primer.

Yet I can suggest four hunting methods that will work very well. First you can shoot them at daybreak, as they leave their night roosting area. Second, you can shoot them in the late evening when the birds begin returning to the roost. Third, you can seek permission to gun them at a cattle or pig feed lot where the birds are causing problems. A fourth possibility would be to set up a stand or blind along a flight route the birds use in getting from roost to feed or vice versa. They'll utilize the same route day after day—until the food supply they're working on is exhausted.

Roost hunting borders on being unbelievable. Once I shot a military reservation, a large stand of evergreens that literally millions of starlings were using as a night roost. They had been using that same roost for years, but I wondered how much longer they'd be able to do so. Their droppings were almost a foot deep under the pines. Every piece of underbrush was long dead, and the evergreens themselves looked as if they too were doomed, this due to the toxicity of the bird's droppings. The stench was worse than any feed lot you've ever visited.

When the starlings stream out in the morning or back in during the late afternoon hours, the volume of shooting possible will boggle the mind of any shotgunner. Say you fire two times with a double gun. While you're reloading, hundreds, sometimes thousands of starlings will pass overhead—all this before you can bring the gun to your shoulder and fire again. The first time I ever tried this type of shooting I figured starlings had to be dumb and unwary. Don't you believe it. Wear camouflage clothing, even set up a blind. If one bird veers away from you, the ones behind play follow the leader—so a million might veer!

Same suggestion goes for gunning a feed lot or intercepting starlings on their flight path from roost to feed and vice versa. Get yourself hidden. Feed lot sport won't bring the type of volume shooting that roost gunning will, but who could complain about firing box after box of shells at a feed lot? With practically any type of hunting these days, including shotgunning any other varmint or game, the number of targets that present themselves for a fair shot is the limiting factor. If you secure the right set up for starling shooting, the limiting factor will be your pocketbook, because you can simply keep shooting and shooting and shooting. Your sore shoulder might also be a factor in limiting how many starlings at which you fire.

Fortunately for our pocketbooks and our shoulders, prime starling shooting like this doesn't last for long. Expect morning shoots with unreal volume shooting to last fifteen minutes maximum at a big roost. Evening volume shooting should last twice as long—maybe thirty minutes max before it's too dark to pick out the targets. No need to arrive early for an afternoon shoot. The starlings typically wait until fading light before they reach the night roost. In the morning they leave at first light, so you'll have to set your alarm for before daybreak. Shooting at feed lots can happen at most any time during the day.

Since there's a tremendous amount of trigger pulling involved, and a great dent is made in the weight of one's shell bag, it pays to use light loads. You'll have to reload. Even millionaires won't shoot factory fodder for long when starlings are involved. The one ounce 12 gauge load is now easy to make up with the Federal 12S3 wad available to reloaders. With many recommended powder charges, this wad and one ounce of shot can result in perfect crimps with Federal *Champion II's,* Peters *Blue Magics,* and Winchester *AA's.* You can even make up little ⅞ ounce 12 gauge reloads. This reduces shot consumption by another 12 percent or so, yet patterns are plenty dense enough at reasonable ranges. If a starling catches one pellet, he's a goner. If you can buy size 10 shot, I'd suggest its use on starlings, but chances are size 9 will be the smallest your dealer will carry, and 9's will do fine. Any shot size larger than 9's has to be a mistake. At thirty yards, using a skeet bored gun, there'll be gaps in a 7½ pattern that several starlings

169

can fly through untouched. Remember, it only takes one pellet to put these little varmints out of commission; so use the smallest size shot you can find.

While the 12 gauge is perfect for gunning starlings, the little 20 gauge is every bit as effective up to about twenty five yards, again utilizing an open bored gun. Here the reloader will find it easy to make up the standard ⅞ ounce 20 gauge loads, as well as reducing the shot charge down to ¾ of an ounce. These'll recoil even less, and the shot in the hopper will go down even slower!

Here are some suggested starling loads, using size 9 shot or smaller. First the 12 gauge. Using the Peters Blue Magic hull, try seventeen grains of DuPont 700X, the Remington 97 primer, that Federal 12S3 wad and one ounce of shot. This load gives 1150 feet per second muzzle velocity. Chamber pressure is quite low at 7500 (LUP), but the load operates my Remington 1100's gas mechanism reliably. If you like DuPont PB powder, try the Blue Magic case with the Federal 209 Primer, 19 grains of PB, the 12S3 wad and one ounce of shot. Muzzle velocity is 1140 fps, with chamber pressure way down to 6800 (LUP). This one delivers minimum recoil, always so important under volume shooting conditions that starlings provide.

Using the Winchester AA hull and one ounce of shot, try 17.5 grains of 700X, the Winchester 209 Primer and the Federal 12S3 wad. Ballistics will be similar to that supplied by the 700X load recommended for the Blue Magic case. Winchester Ball powders tend to be slightly bulkier than Hercules and DuPont shotgun powders, thus they're ideal with some of the wads with shorter columns than the Federal 12S3 provides. I still like to use the Federal 12S3 wad. Reloaders can even use it with the Remington RXP hull to make up little ⅞ ounce 12 gauge loads. Try the RXP case, ⅞ of shot with the Federal 209 Primer, 20 grains of PB with the 12S3. Velocity is 1200 fps and chamber pressure is a mere 7000 (LUP). If you like 700X powder, or only have it on hand, try the 12S3, ⅞ ounce of shot, the RXP case and 17.5 grains of 700X with the Federal 399 Primer. This gives a tad over 1200 fps with chamber pressure only slightly over 7000. There are many loads available for ⅞ ounces of shot for 12 gauge hulls, but so many of them call for the addition of "card" or "fiber" filler wads to be added to the one piece plastic wad column. This creates too much trouble, too much hassle, especially for starling shooters who are trying to put together a great many high quality, low recoiling loads in a minimal period of time.

There are numerous excellent ⅞ ounce target loads one can make up for 20 gauge guns. I consider them excellent choices for anyone who wants to shoot starlings seriously. The Winchester AA case is by far the favorite among reloaders. DuPont 4756 is very good in the 20. Try 19 grains of 4756 in the AA 20 gauge huil, ⅞ ounce of shot, the Federal 209 Primer and the Lage Uniwad. Muzzle velocity is just under

1200 fps. Chamber pressure is 9600 (LUP). With Winchester Ball 473AA powder try ⅞ ounce of shot in the AA 20 gauge case, the Win. 209 Primer, 18 grains of 473AA and the standard Winchester AA 20 gauge wad. This is the standard skeet load—1200 fps, chamber pressure 10,900 (LUP). I also like Hercules Green Dot in the 20 gauge. A light recoiling load is fourteen grains of Green Dot in the AA 20 gauge case, ⅞ ounce of shot, the Winchester 209 Primer and the standard Win. AA 20 gauge wad. Velocity is down to 1155 fps., chamber pressure 10,300.

You'll find that the 12 gauge ⅞ ounce reload recoils less than the ⅞ ounce 20 gauge load. There are a couple of reasons for this. First of all, if both are at the same velocity, chamber pressures tend to be less with the 12, no doubt because there's more space in which the powder can burn. Less pressure is a factor in reduced recoil. A second reason is that a 12 gauge gun is usually heavier than the comparable 20, so the extra gun weight sucks up a bit more of that jar to the shoulder. So—don't sell the loads I have recommended for the ⅞ ounce 12 gauge short. They're dandies, especially for starlings.

Actually, the best 20 gauge reloads for starlings will be the puny ¾ ouncers. These still have plenty of shot pellets at twenty five yards, maybe even slightly beyond. The Remington RXP 20 gauge hull has less capacity than the Win. AA. Consequently, it's the ideal one to consider if you want to make up ¾ ounce 20 gauge loads. Try the RXP gauge hull with 15.5 grains of PB, the Federal 209 Primer, and the standard RXP 20 gauge wad. All the following loads are for ¾ ounce of shot utilizing the Remington RXP 20 gauge hull: Try the RXP 20 wad with 15 grains of Win. 452AA powder and the Win. 209 Primer. With the Win. AA 20 wad try 19 grains of DuPont 4756 and the Win. 209 Primer. With the RXP 20 wad try 15 grains of Unique and the Remington 97 Primer. With the Win. AA 20 wad try 16 grains of Herco and the Win. 209 Primer. You'll be very pleased with these light little ¾ ounce 20 gauge loads—just the ticket for high volume starling shooting.

The 16 gauge hasn't been forgotten, but reloading data on this gauge is slim. The lightest published loads I can find still call for one ounce of shot. Try the Winchester Compression formed 16 gauge hull with 15.5 grains of 700X, the Federal 209 Primer and the Remington R16 wad—one ounce of small shot. Muzzle velocity is 1175. Chamber pressure 9700 (LUP).

The 28 gauge is also excellent for starlings, a trim, light, fast handling gauge that fires ¾ ounce loads. In the Remington SP 28 gauge hull try 17 grains of 4756, the Win. 209 Primer, the Remington SP28 wad and ¾ ounce of shot. Muzzle velocity is 1205 fps, chamber pressure 8400 (LUP). With the Federal 28 gauge Target case try 17.5 grains of 4756, the Win. 209 Primer, the Remington SP28 wad and ¾ ounce of shot—for 1200 fps and 8200 (LUP). With the 28 gauge Win. AA hull try 19 grains of Win. Ball 571, the CCI 209 Primer and the standard Win. AA 28 gauge wad. This produces the standard 1200 fps skeet load—at 10,300 (LUP).

Even the puny .410 is a possibility, though I'm not an advocate of this gauge (actually caliber) for anything other than starlings. One pellet, as mentioned before, will usually do the number on a starling. The .410 skeet factory stuff with half an ounce of 9's is fine. Factory ballistics can be duplicated by using the Winchester AA .410 case, the Win. 209 AA .410 wad, half an ounce of 9's and 13.5 grains of Winchester 296 Ball Powder. The ¾ ounce three inch .410 factory load is another possibility, though the 28 gauge ¾ ounce load will give far superior patterns. Reloaders can make up ¹¹⁄₁₆ ounce three inch .410 loads by using the three inch Win. Compression Formed Hull, their 209 primer, the Winchester WAA41 wad and 13.5 grains of 296.

Starlings didn't arrive in this country until March 6, 1890. At least that date marked the first successful introduction of this foreign species. One Eugene Scheifflin introduced eighty starlings to New York's Central Park on that date. A year later, April 25, 1891, Mr. Scheifflin brought over forty more. As early as 1891 starlings were in residence on Staten Island. By 1896 they had spread to Brooklyn. By 1898 they were seen as far away as Stamford, Connecticut and Plainfield, New Jersey. Now starlings are everywhere. Why?

When a species is introduced to a new land, it either quickly dies out or takes hold with remarkable quickness. If any new species successfully takes hold, nature's control factors and the bird's predators have been left behind—in the old country! Their numbers are likely to blossom like they never did in the land to which they were originally indigenous.

Once the starling did take hold in America, it was a good bet their population would mushroom to current levels. The bird is perfectly suited to survival. His nature is to be pugnacious. That means he's willing to fight for the best nesting spots and for at least his fair share of the food that's available. The starling is muscular and powerful with the physical characteristics of a crow. He's also been described as tough and wiry. His bill is long and strong, a most effective weapon in either offense or defense. This bird is very brave around other birds, especially if the starling feels it can be dominant. Conversely, starlings are very wary around creatures they know they can't lick.

There's little question that the starling is responsible for the tremendous reduction in the numbers of several songbird species. Starlings are simply so aggressive, pugnacious and persistent in choosing nest sites that they force other species out. They're also nest destroyers with regard to other bird species, eating eggs outright or breaking them with their beaks. Thus the decline in bluebirds, house wrens, woodpeckers, flickers and others.

Some speculate that vast numbers of spring starlings can affect the mast supply. They feed the young staminate flowers of hickory, oak and beech. Enough starlings can vastly reduce the fall supply of acorns, hickory and beech nuts.

Starlings do eat insects. As long as flocks of starlings are plentiful, it's unlikely that insects will reach plague proportions. The bird's scientific name is *Sturnus vulgaris*. While the starling is black overall in color, it has iridescent purple neck feathers on top of the black, with iridescent blue and violet wing coverts. Some body feathers are iridescent green over black. The bird's body is flecked with small whitish spots. The yellow beak is relatively long, and very strong. The tail is short, making it easy to distinguish in flight from grackles and red-winged blackbirds. Starlings are very swift flyers, adding to their value as a shotgun target.

Another reason the starling gets along so well is that the bird can subsist on about any food there is. Its first love might be fruits and seeds, but starlings can subsist on such a wide variety of foodstuffs that they can get by in horrible weather conditions when other birds can't.

Nesting starlings will be more solitary compared to the huge flocks which congregate for migration and in the wintering areas, but starlings sometimes nest in fairly large flocks. Nests might be in tree or cliff cavities, house eaves, church steeples, just about anywhere. The nests contain three to six eggs, and both parents share in incubation duties, as well as helping to rear the young. Many starlings raise two broods every season.

There's little question that the country is stuck with starlings. Shotgunners can make the best of it by hunting these varmints at every opportunity. No amount of hunting will ever have any affect on the overall population of these vulgar critters, but anyone willing to invest time and effort in shooting starlings is going to improve his wing-shooting skills by a marked degree. At this point in time starlings offer the only limitless shotgun shooting target in America.

Camouflaged hunter and Remington 1100 auto-loader. This gun is ideal for a lot of varmint hunting.

CHAPTER 15

Shotguns for Crows, Pigeons and Starlings

If you've read through the shotgun section this far, you know I'm sold on gas operated semi-autoloaders for this type of shooting. It wasn't always that way. There was a time when I couldn't get them to work reliably with my reloads. I've since discovered the reloads were the problem, not the gas guns. Takes most reloaders a couple of years to realize that the only effective way to produce quality loads is to follow recommended reloading recipes to the letter. Not only is this the only way to produce safe loads, it's the only way to produce ones that'll work reliably, especially in semi-autos.

Beginning reloaders produce some sorry looking fodder. But so what, they think, it'll shoot. Most of these shells do fire, but the tyro is incorrectly satisfied with producing reloads that are vastly inferior to factory ammunition, just because his junk is cheaper. Only those who reload long enough come around to realizing that high quality reloads can be produced, and that shells coming out of a basement reloading machine can be every bit as good as shells from the huge factory presses that spit out Winchesters, Remingtons and Federals by the thousands. As far as I'm concerned, quality reloads are the only ones worth producing. Any sacrifice in quality isn't worth the time and effort, regardless of the money savings involved.

For my money the Remington 1100 is the best gun around for shooting crows, pest pigeons and starlings—a 12 gauge. They're not cheap, but their price won't leave you with your mouth agape, either. A full choke is the best for crows and pigeons. I like shorter barrels. One year Remington offered a 26 inch full choke barrel, which I consider the perfect length for a pump or auto used for hunting. Luckily, I was fortunate to get one. Rumors circulate that the 26 inch full 1100 barrel may be offered again. Let's hope so—for the good of the rest of the shotgunning fraternity. I have another 26 inch barrel for my 1100's, formerly a skeet choke. I sent it off to Jesse Briley (Briley Manufacturing, 1035 Gessner C, Houston, TX 77055). He drilled and tapped it for his excellent screw-in chokes. Now I have eight different ones, with constrictions of .005 (skeet), .010, .015, .020, .025, .030, .035 and .040 (extra full). When starling shooting I take the barrel for the screw-in chokes, usually using the .005 skeet, but occasionally a tighter choke—depending upon the range I'm encountering the little black birds.

The U.S. Repeating Arms Co. makes a 12 gauge auto-loader already threaded for Winchokes (screw-in chokes). This one comes with a 28 inch barrel, and is dubbed their Model 1500. It doesn't have the great reliability reputation among experienced clay target shooters that the 1100 has.

Smith & Wesson's Model 1000 auto-loader, though introduced recently, is developing an excellent reputation. In 1982 S&W announced their screw-in choke version for this one—called the Multi-Choke system. I feel more and more gun companies are going to be offering screw-in choke options in the future.

The Winchester Super X, though a fine consideration, is no longer offered. This could be an excellent used gun bargain. Both Benelli and Beretta have excellent auto-loaders.

The pump gun man couldn't make a better choice than Remington's long lived and reliable 870. Produced since 1949, sales are approaching four million. U.S. Repeating Arms has their Model 1300 pump, and it comes with Winchokes. Smith & Wesson has their Model 3000 pump—and it now comes with their Multi-Choke screw-in system. The Browning BPS pump is superb.

In the over-and-under line I like the 3200 Remington over and under because it weighs plenty and sucks up abusive recoil. Perhaps an even better consideration, though, is one of the Winchester 101's with screw-in chokes. These are versatile two holers, and you can use them for a great deal more than merely crows, pest pigeons and starlings. The Browning Citori is also in the unbeatable class. This one has plenty of heft and weight for absorbing recoil. I have one fitted for Jesse Briley's screw-in chokes, so it's perfect medicine for the three varmints covered in this shotgunning chapter. Finally, there's the Ruger Red Label. Available for several years in 20 gauge only, this snappy looking and fast handling over-and-under is finally available in 12 gauge. I can't

Browning 20 gauge Citori *and array of Briley screw-in chokes.*

wait to get my hands on one. Soon as I fire it a few rounds I'm going to send it off to Jesse Briley for a set of his screw-in chokes.

There's little question that many who want to hunt crows, pest pigeons and starlings will not buy a new gun. They'll use one they already have. Hopefully it won't be "any ole gun." To be effective on crows, pest pigeons and starlings, at least some degree of specialty should be considered. The suggestions in this chapter will help you make the proper choice.

APPENDIX

Binoculars

Bushnell Optical
2828 Foothill Blvd.
Pasadena, CA 91107

Swarovski
Strieter Corp.
2100 18th Ave.
Rock Island, IL 61201

Jason/Empire
9200 Cody
Overland Park, KS 66214

Swift Instruments
952 Dorchester Ave.
Boston, MA 02125

Ziess
444 Fifth Ave.
New York, NY 10018

E. Leitz
Rockleigh, NJ 07647

Tasco
P.O. Box 520080
Miami, FL 33152

Custom Barrel Makers

Christy Gun Works
875 57th Street
Sacramento, CA 95819

Douglas Barrels
55-4 Big Tyler Road
Charleston, WV 25312

Federal Firearms
Box 145
Oakdale, PA 15071

Hart Rifle Barrels
R.D. #2
Lafayette, NY 13084

David Huntington
RFD #1, Box 23
Heber City, UT 84032

Nu-Line Guns
1053 Caulkshill Road
Harvester, MO 63303

Ed Shilen Rifles
205 Metropark Blvd.
Ennis, TX 75119

Titus Barrels
R.F.D. #1, Box 23
Heber City, UT 84032

Camouflage masks

Ben Rogers Lee
Coffeeville, AL 36524

Penns Woods
19 West Pittsburgh St.
Delmont, PA 15626

Calls

Burnham Bros.
Marble Falls, TX 78654

Custom Stock Makers

Brown Precision
P.O. Box 270W
Los Molinos, CA 96055
(916) 384-2506

Bob Brownell
Main & Third
Montezuma, Iowa 50171
(glass bedding)

Reinhart Fajen
Box 338
Warsaw, MO 65355
(314) 438-5111

Paul Jaeger
211 Leedom Street
Jenkintown, PA 19046
(215) 884-6920

Jim Peightal
#6 Eighth St.
Ernest, PA 15739
(412) 349-5216
Six Enterprises
6564 Hidden Creek Dr.
San Jose, CA 95120
(408) 268-8296

Brent Unberger
Sportsman's Haven
R.D. #4
Cambridge, OH 43725

Rests

Cravners Gun Shop
1627 Fifth Ave.
Ford City, PA 16226
(Micro Rest shooting stand)

Harris Engineering
Barlow, KY 42024
(Harris Bipod Rest)

MTM Molded Products Co.
Dayton, OH 45414
(walking stick/rest)

Munitions

Godfrey Reloading Supply
Box 688
City Limits Road
Brighton, IL 62012

Homer Cleckler
3774 Spring Dr.
Huntsville, TX 77340

Cleaning Rods

Taylor & Robbins
Box 164
Rixford, PA 16745

Publications
Shotgun News
Snell Publishing Inc.
Hastings, NE 68901

Gun World
P.O. Box HH
Capistrano Beach, CA 92624

Chokes

Briley Manufacturing
1035 Gessner Court
Houston, TX 77055
(screw-in chokes)

Other **Stone Wall Press** Books for Hunters

Keeping Warm and Dry, by Harry Roberts
128 pages, paperback, illustrations $7.95 list

Don't get caught unprepared on your next hunting trip! Sudden cold, or drenching rain often hit the careless. Let Harry Roberts tell you how he would prepare for a hunting trip in any part of the country. Solid what-works advice, field tested techniques and no-nonsense looks at today's fibers and gear.

Goose Hunting, by Charles Cadieux
208 pages, hardcover, photographs, $16.95 list

Stories of personal experience, facts about goose management, goose hunting and watching are interwoven to make for an entertaining and informative book. Cadieux has made the outdoors his life—as a game warden, and an outdoors writer. "The author has a way of making his point, instructing his reader, and entertaining him, all at the same time." *Field and Stream.* Goose hunting from Quebec to Mexico, and solid advice along the way.

The Natural World Cookbook—Complete Gourmet Meals from Wild Edibles, by Joe Freitus
301 pages, illustrations, index, hardcover, $25.00 list

Complete and comprehensive, this is a twenty-year collection of proven gourmet recipes for wild plants, fish, fowl and game. Hundreds of recipes are carefully presented with clear how-to-find illustrations. Freitus has taken up where Euell Gibbons left off. "Everything for the wild foods connoisseur!" *Scot Wildlife News.*

These are the Endangered, by Charles Cadieux
240 pages, photographs, and illustrations by Bob Hines. Clothbound, $16.95 list.

A dramatic look at the plight of our endangered wildlife, along with current legislation and efforts to save them through agencies, parks, zoos, and organizations. Thoroughly researched, well written. "... highly recommended for sportsmen, who have a responsibility to protect wildlife." *Sports Afield.*

The Sporting Shotgun, by Robin Marshall-Ball
A User's Handbook
176 pages, photographs, illustrations, maps, hardcover, $23.95 list.

An important international reference to shotgunning in North America, Britain, and Europe. Marshall-Ball gives the shooter a history of shotgunning, the principles of shotgun mechanics, and hints on the points to watch when purchasing a shotgun. Fully illustrated chapters discuss game and distribution throughout North America and Europe. Indexed.